ROUTLEDGE LIBRARY EDITIONS: LIBRARY AND INFORMATION SCIENCE

Volume 94

SERVING END-USERS IN SCI-TECH LIBRARIES

SERVING END-USERS IN SCI-TECH LIBRARIES

Edited by
ELLIS MOUNT

Routledge
Taylor & Francis Group
LONDON AND NEW YORK

First published in 1984 by The Haworth Press, Inc.

This edition first published in 2020
by Routledge
2 Park Square, Milton Park, Abingdon, Oxon OX14 4RN

and by Routledge
52 Vanderbilt Avenue, New York, NY 10017

Routledge is an imprint of the Taylor & Francis Group, an informa business

© 1984 The Haworth Press, Inc.

All rights reserved. No part of this book may be reprinted or reproduced or utilised in any form or by any electronic, mechanical, or other means, now known or hereafter invented, including photocopying and recording, or in any information storage or retrieval system, without permission in writing from the publishers.

Trademark notice: Product or corporate names may be trademarks or registered trademarks, and are used only for identification and explanation without intent to infringe.

British Library Cataloguing in Publication Data
A catalogue record for this book is available from the British Library

ISBN: 978-0-367-34616-4 (Set)
ISBN: 978-0-429-34352-0 (Set) (ebk)
ISBN: 978-0-367-36441-0 (Volume 94) (hbk)
ISBN: 978-0-367-36445-8 (Volume 94) (pbk)
ISBN: 978-0-429-34610-1 (Volume 94) (ebk)

Publisher's Note
The publisher has gone to great lengths to ensure the quality of this reprint but points out that some imperfections in the original copies may be apparent.

Disclaimer
The publisher has made every effort to trace copyright holders and would welcome correspondence from those they have been unable to trace.

Serving End-Users in Sci-Tech Libraries

Ellis Mount, Editor

The Haworth Press
New York

Serving End-Users in Sci-Tech Libraries has also been published as *Science & Technology Libraries,* Volume 5, Number 1, Fall 1984.

© 1984 by The Haworth Press, Inc. All rights reserved. No part of this book may be reproduced or utilized in any form or by any means, electronic or mechanical, including photocopying, microfilm and recording, or by any information storage and retrieval system, without permission in writing from the publisher. Printed in the United States of America.

The Haworth Press, Inc., 28 East 22 Street, New York, NY 10010

Library of Congress Cataloging in Publication Data
Main entry under title:

Serving end-users in sci-tech libraries.

    Also published as Science & technology libraries, volume 5, number 1, fall 1984.
    Bibliography: p.
    1. Technical libraries—Technological innovations. 2. Scientific libraries—Technological innovations. 3. Science—Information services. 4. Technology—Information services. 5. Information storage and retrieval systems—Science. 6. Information storage and retrieval systems—Technology. I. Mount, Ellis.
Z675.T3S43 1984   025.5'2765'02854   84-10789
ISBN 0-86656-327-X

Serving End-Users in Sci-Tech Libraries

Science & Technology Libraries
Volume 5, Number 1

CONTENTS

Introduction	xi
Database Development and End-User Searching: Exxon Research and Engineering Company	1
R. S. Lescohier	
M. A. Lavin	
M. K. Landsberg	
Introduction	1
Phase I—User Needs and Databases	3
Phase II—Online End-User Training	10
Conclusion	14
Teaching University Student End-Users about Online Searching	17
Sandra N. Ward	
Laura M. Osegueda	
Introduction	17
Experiences at Stanford University	19
Experiences at San Jose State University	22
Summary of Experiences at Both Institutions	25
Implementation and Funding	26
Conclusions	29
Managing Effective Information Services for End-Users in Academic Sci-Tech Libraries	33
Arleen N. Somerville	
Introduction	33
Communication	34
Marketing Information Services	35

Information Instructional Programs	40
Information Programs	41
Collection Development	45
Staff	46

American Petroleum Institute's Machine-Aided Indexing and Searching Project — 49
E. H. Brenner
J. H. Lucey
C. L. Martinez
Adel Meleka

Introduction	49
The Plan	50
The Machine-Aided Indexing Project: Description and Current Status	51
Machine-Aided Searching: A Proposal	57
Summary	62

Preparation of a Slide/Tape Program for Biological Abstracts: Harvard University — 63
Eva S. Jonas

Introduction	63
Background	64
Starting with the Script	64
Production of Slides	65
Taping the Narration	66
Reviewing	66
Use of the Slide/Tape	67

Increasing End-User Awareness of Library Services Through Promotion: Grumman Aerospace Corporation — 69
Claude E. Gibson
Harold B. Smith

Introduction	69
Production of the Videotape	71
Equipment Needed	76

NEW REFERENCE WORKS IN SCIENCE AND TECHNOLOGY — 79
Robert G. Krupp, Editor

SCI-TECH ONLINE   **101**
    Ellen Nagle, Editor

National Online Meeting Held   101
Database News   102
Search System News   103

SCI-TECH IN REVIEW   **105**
    Suzanne Fedunok, Editor

Scientific Publishing   105
Documentary Information in Industry   107
Information for Management   108
Gatekeeper Reconsidered   109
Cycle Times on Information   109

SCI-TECH COLLECTIONS   **111**
    Tony Stankus, Editor

A Brief Fermentation Biotechnology Guide to Biochemical Engineering, Industrial Microbiology and Fermentation Literature   **113**
    Will Jarvis

Subject Guide   113
"Bioengineering" and "Genetic Engineering"   114
Narrower Core and Wider Applications Polarity   115
Biotechnology's "Close Relations" Food and Beverage Microbiology, Biomass Conversion, and Sewage Processing   116
Further Indexing Considerations   117
Conclusion   118
Selected Bibliography   119
Appendix I   121

INTRODUCTION

Serving End-Users in Sci-Tech Libraries

In recent years much has been written about the informational problems of the end-user, a term which to most librarians means simply those who use the services of libraries and information centers. Those interested in science and technology have many problems to face, one of which is the fast-growing technical literature and another is the complexities of some of the tools and products needed for retrieving information in these disciplines. Therefore it seems appropriate to devote an issue to the various ways in which sci-tech libraries are meeting the needs of our end-users.

The corporate scene is dealt with in the paper by R. S. Lescohier, M. A. Lavin and M. K. Landsberg; they discuss how the Exxon Research and Engineering Company has met users' needs for certain proprietary data by a two-phase project which included developing a new in-house database and providing special online search instruction courses for engineers.

The academic outlook is presented in two papers. The first, by Sandra Ward and Laura Osegueda, describes ways of introducing the process of online searching to science students at Stanford University and San Jose State University. The other paper, by Arleen Somerville, shows how many aspects of sci-tech library management relate to meeting the needs of end-users; various user groups' needs are described as well as many ways in which academic sci-tech libraries can best serve these groups.

The viewpoint of the producer of a major database is given in the paper which was written by E. H. Brenner, J. H. Lucey, C. L. Martinez and A. Meleka and which describes how the American Petroleum Institute is experimenting with an automated indexing system which would be aimed at developing a more friendly system for users doing online searches.

Two entirely different uses for audiovisual products have led to two papers describing the production of these tools. In the first Eva Jonas tells of her work in producing a slide/tape program for orienting undergraduate science students at Harvard University in their use of *Biological Abstracts*. The other paper, by Claude Gibson and Harold Smith, describes their project in preparing a videotape orientation program for use in familiarizing employees of the Grumman Aerospace Corporation with library services.

In this issue we are pleased to add one more special section to our regular features. The new one, entitled Sci-Tech Collections, will present papers dealing with the key literature on certain sci-tech topics of current interest. It will be edited by Tony Stankus, a member of the Editorial Board. The first paper, by Will Jarvis, deals with the literature of biotechnology. Anyone wishing to contribute such a paper for future issues of this journal should contact Mr. Stankus at the address found in the introduction to this new section.

Ellis Mount, Editor

Database Development and End-User Searching: Exxon Research and Engineering Company

R. S. Lescohier
M. A. Lavin
M. K. Landsberg

ABSTRACT. Exxon Research and Engineering Company's experience in providing a complete storage and retrieval system, manual and online, for a group of Exxon engineers is detailed. The two-phase project for providing direct end-user access to proprietary information involved a collection audit, a user survey, document collection microfilming and organization, database construction, and end-user training in the use of indexes and online interactive searching. Key factors for the success of this project were an information intermediary assigned to the engineering division, the availability of flexible information systems, and the direct involvement of engineers and engineering management.

INTRODUCTION

Research and Engineering Information Services (REIS), provides technical information to Exxon's scientists and engineers. It

---

Karen Landsberg is a Section Head responsible for Information Systems in Research and Engineering Information Services at Exxon Research and Engineering Company, P.O. Box 101, Florham Park, NJ 07932. She has a BS in chemistry from Drexel University and an MS in physical chemistry from Rutgers University.

Rosary S. Lescohier is at present an Information Staff Analyst in REIS at Exxon Research and Engineering Company. She has a BA in history from the College of Saint Elizabeth.

Margaret A. Lavin is an Information Analyst in REIS at Exxon Research and Engineering Company's Florham Park Information Center. She holds a BS in chemistry from Montclair State College and an MLS from Rutgers University.

Acknowledgement should also be given to other Exxon employees who contributed to the success of the project: Donald J. Gallo, John Hack, Linda J. Herman, Nancy Kafarski, Gilbert D. Lee and Patricia A. Lorenz.

© 1984 by The Haworth Press, Inc. All rights reserved.

operates three major information centers serving basic research, chemical, product, and engineering organizations and affiliates.

Although the work and information needs of these groups are diverse, all users have become increasingly aware of the value of information and of the potential of computer access to information resources. For some time, end users have been provided with direct access to information resources through the development of specialized databases and online searching.

Some of REIS's programs for developing end-user online searching of external databases have been reported in the literature. In 1979, an experiment conducted in conjunction with Drexel University evaluated an intermediary search system—Individual Instruction for Data Access (IIDA).[1] The IIDA system was designed to expedite end-user searching by providing instruction, assistance, and diagnostics. In the experiment, both scientists and engineers were trained to search Compendex and NTIS with and without IIDA. The experiment generated a high level of interest, and some Exxon scientists and engineers, with additional training, continue to search on their own.

REIS's searching staff has also developed and taught courses in online searching for chemists.[2] These projects have focused on public chemical and petrochemical database such as CA Search, APILIT, and PROMT. REIS also taught some end users at remote Exxon sites that have no technical searching staff. Again, the end users were primarily chemists, and the emphasis was on external databases. Although only a small number of end users continued to search after these projects, it was concluded that online searching is a valuable tool that should be placed at the disposal of scientists and engineers.

In general, published information is of greatest interest to scientists and proprietary material of most significance to engineers. Providing end users with access to proprietary information is an even greater challenge than providing access to published material because needs have to be defined, collections of information must be organized, and appropriate databases must be constructed. And, if the information is to be computerized, a system must be developed.

Within Exxon, REIS began using indexes from computerized databases for access to formal technical reports in 1963, and in 1970 we applied them to organizing company correspondence.[3] The technical reports system was available in official Reports Centers throughout Exxon, and the correspondence system was widely distributed to clients. More recently, in keeping with the general trend towards information decentralization and individual access to information in or near end users' offices and laboratories, both the technical reports and correspondence system have been made very widely accessible via online interactive searching.

This paper focuses on some of REIS's experiences with providing local access to proprietary information for end users at our engineering facility. The specific project reported here involved a particular engineering unit and was implemented in two phases. Phase I defined users' needs, organized the unit's material, developed a customized database, and trained engineers to use indexes and the source document collection on paper and microfiche. Phase II organized an online training course for the engineers in the division. Thus, a complete storage and retrieval system was developed that enabled the engineers to identify and retrieve for themselves proprietary information using either manual or online methods as best suited their requirements.

PHASE I—USER NEEDS AND DATABASES

Engineering Division Background

One engineering division within Exxon requested that REIS review and evaluate their access to information. The group was keenly aware of the potential of computer databases and was anxious to improve their access to existing divisional information.

The scope of the work done by this division is varied, including research and development, troubleshooting for affiliates, original project design, and review of detailed design work done by Exxon and contractor organizations. This results in most of their work being documented in letters, memoranda, specifications, and telexes. Although the published literature is important to them, they have a greater need for access to their own proprietary documents.

Their existing system for handling proprietary documents comprised four distinct divisional files: one set of files for design projects, arranged by affiliate location; another for R&D projects; a set of general technical files, arranged by equipment, process-unit names, etc.; and a smaller file of miscellaneous documents. Since there was no cross referencing, an engineer interested in a single subject could have to search all four files to collect relevant data.

There was also no one individual responsible for the maintenance of the file structure.

Thus, the system was generally viewed as inefficient, and few engineers had confidence in it. This lack of confidence further complicated the situation because fewer and fewer engineers submitted materials to be included in the divisional file, and the integrity of the system diminished rapidly. Because of their knowledge of the technical applications of computing, familiarity with online searching of the published literature, and awareness of the database systems available within REIS, the division's engineers looked to computerization as a possible answer to their problem, and they contacted REIS for assistance.

REIS Involvement

REIS was aware of the need to increase end-user access to their centrally maintained databases and looked upon this as an opportunity to increase local access to and awareness of information systems.

The project began with interviews with a series of engineers who had been assigned the task of overseeing the implementation of a new system. The interviews consisted of discussions of the existing system and a gathering of their ideas on how they would like to see it improved. The interviews were followed by an audit of all the files to determine the actual size of the collection and the variety of classification schemes used.

Proposal

REIS prepared a proposal for the division based on this evaluation. The proposal included an evaluation of the existing system, recommendations for improvement, and a cost estimate for the project. There were three specific recommendations for resolving the situation: (1) implementation of a customized online bibliographic database, (2) less dependency upon the engineers to maintain the system, and (3) more detailed indexing of documents in the collection.

The recommended database could be built taking full advantage of an indexing and online searching system already available within REIS. The system has the flexibility to generate customized indexes as well as provide online access. The total system was compatible with the information handling and computing systems being promoted within the company and had the flexibility to meet the needs expressed by this group.

The proposal also recommended that a mini-information center staffed by REIS personnel be located among the division's offices. It became evident during the evaluation period that a new computerized system alone was not the answer to the existing problem. Dedicated attention to the maintenance of the information collection as well as the system was required. Justification for assigning REIS staff to this mini-information center was based on this staff member keeping the division's information handling systems compatible with the rest of the company and also being informed of the latest innovations in information technology. In addition, this staff member's responsibility would be keyed to information handling and would not be diverted to other divisional duties, which was part of the existing problem. Economic justification for staffing the mini-information center was based on the division's ability to shift to this person all information associated functions previously handled by others. Thus the division did not have to increase staff to implement the proposal.

The proposal recommended that engineer participation was essential for initial implementation and continuing input to the new database. Initial participation required the engineers in the division to cull existing files and fill out document input forms (Figures 1 and 2) using a list of controlled keywords. Continuing participation required the engineers to use this input form for all new documents and to be trained in the use of indexes and the online interactive database.

Other recommendations were the extensive microfilming of documents in the divisional collection and the purchase of equipment for reading and printing microfiche. The proposal was accepted and implementation of the plan began in January 1982. In addition, an engineer in the division was assigned to coordinate the project and act as liaison with REIS.

Computer System

The project's objective was to provide rapid, comprehensive retrieval, while reducing filing time and saving space. An in-house computer system met these needs. The program has several modules and supports databases both for batch reporting and online interactive searching. The most extensive application of the system has

Figure 1

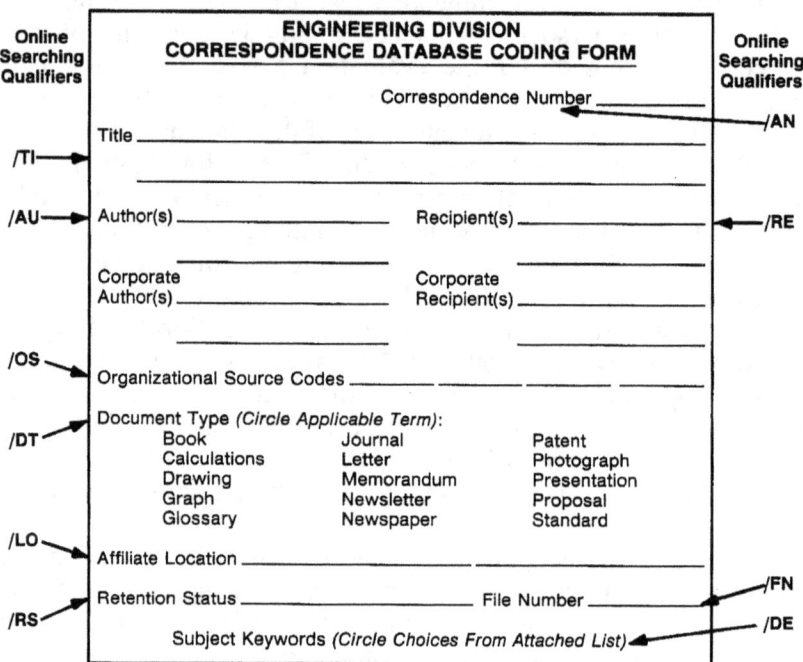

been bibliographic databases, and that was the application required here.

All documents received for inclusion in these databases are issued a unique reference number and are assigned a meaningful title and other indexing elements as required by the client. This bibliographic and subject information is input to the database, and the documents are microfiched.

One of the system's products is batch-report indexes, which issue periodically. These batch indexes provide retrieval on several access points, e.g., subjects (Key-Word-In-Context (KWIC) index based on title or abstract words), personal or corporate authors, personal or corporate recipients, reference number, and any other assigned indexing elements. Since all index formats contain a document's reference number, documents need to be filed only once (paper or microfiche), in reference-number order, thus eliminating multiple filing.

The online system used for searching the databases provides the advantages presently afforded by publicly available systems.

Databases and Retrieval Systems

During the collection audit, it became evident that many of the documents contained in the division's collection were formal Exxon technical reports, which were already in a database. Thus, the division could use two pertinent databases: a technical reports database and a correspondence database.

The technical reports database contains reports, generated by Exxon affiliates worldwide, that cover subjects such as petroleum refining and products, synthetic fuels, engineering, and chemistry. The structure of this database and its products already have been described.[3]

The division's correspondence database contains the documents that remained after culling, and new documents are added on a continuing basis. The majority portion of the documents indexed are let-

Figure 2

ENGINEERING DIVISION SUBJECT KEYWORD LIST

Circle Applicable Terms:

Materials	Equipment	Incidents	Processes	Properties
Ammonia	Compressors	Blast	Alkylation	Buoyancy
Asphalt	Fans	Boilover	Aromatization	Density
Chloride	Pumps	Contamination	Desalination	Permeability
Coal	Turbines	Corrosion	Deoiling	Porosity
Concrete	Valves	Earthquakes		
Glass		Ignition		
Oxygen				
Paint				

ters, memoranda, and telexes, but engineering design specifications and calculations, manuals, and published literature of importance to the division are also indexed.

The unique reference number assigned to each document in this database identifies the document, the issuing group, the year of issue, and whether it is an issued or received document. The author's original title is used, but it is amplified when necessary. Authors and recipients and their corporate affiliations are included and are individually searchable in both the indexes and the online searching system.

Database Customization

In keeping with this engineering division's need for divisionally specific indexing, additional indexing fields were used in this database: subject keywords selected by the engineers from a controlled list, a document-type identifier, retention status information, the affiliate location associated with the document, the original file number or classification code used for older documents, and codes to segment the database by major time periods and general subjects. A sample record, including all of these fields, appears in Figure 3. These fields are all searchable in both the indexes and the online searching system.

As mentioned, the computer system used to build this database was already being used centrally to capture all company correspondence and all Exxon technical reports. The correspondence of this particular division is included in the same database used by other company divisions, but the indexing codes used in the database enable this group to search only their own portion of the file when this is appropriate.

Phase I Conclusion

Upon completion of Phase I of this project, the division's correspondence database contained approximately 7,000 records, and it is being added to at the rate of 2,000 records per year. A user's manual was written to describe the complete document collection, instruct engineers in the use of the indexes, and outline the details of the system's operation.

A preliminary review by the division's management projected a possible savings of 2.5% of an engineer's work week due to im-

Figure 3
SAMPLE RECORD—CORRESPONDENCE DATABASE

          (Year) (Organization) (Sequential Number)

CORRESPONDENCE NUMBER	—82 STD 154
TITLE	—Siting and Design of Blast Resistant Buildings in Petroleum and Chemical Plants
AUTHORS	—A.L. Watts and J. Swensen
CORPORATE AUTHOR	—Safety Technology Division
RECIPIENTS	—L.K. O'Leary and L. Jackson
CORPORATE RECIPIENT	—Civil Engineering Division
SUBJECT KEYWORDS	—Safety; Fire Protection; Concrete; Earthquake; Building; Seismic; Construction; Site Selection
DOCUMENT TYPE	—Memorandum
AFFILIATE LOCATION	—Baytown, TX
RETENTION STATUS	—1987–ALW *(Year and Initials of Reviewer)*
ORGANIZATIONAL SOURCE CODES	—STD *(Safety Technology Division)* CED *(Civil Engineering Division)*

proved access to information provided in Phase I. For this division, this savings alone corresponds to $150k/year. Based on these results division management gave the go ahead for Phase II, which included instruction of end-users in online searching.

PHASE II—ONLINE END-USER TRAINING

Goals and Design

The online training for the division was designed to maximize individual training and minimize engineers' time from their other work. Class size was limited to fifteen engineers, and session assignments were based on individuals' technical backgrounds and availabilities. Although the sessions were identical in structure, subject emphasis depended upon the backgrounds of the attendees. Limiting the sessions to two hours enabled engineering management to encourage total divisional attendance.

The training session was designed to be a basic introduction to online searching, to the structure of the technical reports and correspondence databases, and to the online system. The goal was to teach the engineers to structure search statements and execute simple commands. Further advanced instruction, on an individual basis, was available upon request.

Searching Tools

Three searching tools were prepared for use during the training sessions and for future reference. They consisted of a user's manual, a quick-reference guide, and customized searching aids. The divisional correspondence and technical reports databases were emphasized during the training sessions and in these materials.

The user's manual contains instructions for searching the proprietary databases. Section one is a primer for the novice searcher. It describes basic functions, including logging onto the system, correcting typing errors, and terminating communication within the system. It also explains the fundamentals of online searching, including some simple examples. Section two discusses the more sophisticated searching techniques that can be used to obtain the most relevant records. The remaining sections contain detailed descriptions of the correspondence and reports databases. As registered manual recipients, participants receive updates, including notices regarding new databases and new system features.

The quick reference guide consists of information extracted from the user's manual and is printed on an eleven-by-seventeen-inch piece of cardboard folded twice for handy access. It was designed for fast use at the terminals. The guide includes instructions for getting on and off the system, hotline numbers with names to call in case of questions, summarized database descriptions, searching tips, and some of the more useful commands.

Customized searching aids were developed exclusively for use by this division. They illustrate searching techniques and database features using divisional documents and typical search queries. These included the following:

—Correspondence Database Diagram

> Since the divisional correspondence database represented only a portion of the central database constructed and maintained by REIS for all company divisions, it was necessary to illustrate the database's total content and their own database's relative position within it.

—Annotated Correspondence Input Form

> The document input form, which is used by the engineers for submitting documents to the system, was annotated with the searching qualifiers for each field (see Figure 1). This aid linked indexing input with searching output and became a key to explaining the online database's Basic Index.

—Field Qualifier Table

> A table of all field qualifiers, abbreviations for the database fields, identifying which are available for searching and printing and including brief explanations, was also supplied. This table specifically isolated all fields in the Basic Index.

—Command Table

> A page of selected commands with simple examples pertinent to these end-users' specific needs was included. Among these were commands for single and multicharacter truncation, commands for searching the author field, and commands for reviewing search strategy.

—Print Format Illustrations

A typical search record was explained in detail, and instructions on possible printing formats were given. Particular emphasis was placed on the most concise choices.

—Sample Search Questions

Five search questions, tailored to the backgrounds of the engineers present at each training session, were distributed. For example, all were asked to find the documents that they had authored. There were also two subject-related questions. One was designed to generate a small number of references; the other was designed to result in an unmanageable number of hits requiring the engineers to limit their search strategies. The remaining search questions involved the use of the various field qualifiers.

In addition, logsheets were distributed to be completed every time the engineer used the online system. These sheets aided REIS in determining the volume of engineering use of the system, asking for the date of each search session, how long it lasted, the cost, and which databases were searched.

Instructors and Facilities

Five REIS instructors were present during each session. Four were members of the searching staff, and one was the REIS contact assigned to the division.

The training sessions started in a special training room containing a terminal with an overhead display screen. An online demonstration was done during each session. The terminal used during the training sessions was identical to terminals available in most engineers' offices throughout Exxon. It was considered a great advantage that the division's online databases were available through equipment and systems with which the engineers were already familiar.

Training Session Structure

Each training session had three separate parts. The first part was a thirty-minute oral presentation, the second a thirty-minute online demonstration, and the third an hour-long hands-on practice session. The first two parts were held in the training room. The third was held in the offices of those engineers who had terminals.

The oral presentation covered the searching system and an overview of the structures of the two databases. This explanation was enhanced through the use of all the searching tools discussed previously.

In the online demonstration, the engineers were able to view the entire session from beginning to end. They were shown how to log onto the system, select the file of their choice, and proceed with the search. They were shown how to formulate search strategies and to use commands to search the online dictionary, review search strategies, and truncate terms. Searching the Basic Index, using individual field qualifiers, and the Boolean operators (And, Or, And Not) were explained and demonstrated at some length.

Once the search was completed, document citations were viewed in various print formats. In addition, instructions were given for printing references from previous search statements, as well as skipping references already printed and viewing subsequent ones. The participants were then shown how to log off the system, obtain the cost of the session, and complete the logsheet.

Groups consisting of three engineers and one searcher were formed for the hands-on session. Backgrounds and interests were considered during this session also. While the instructor looked on, each engineer worked a search problem. Once through three questions, they logged off and then reentered the system. Everyone had a chance to practice the procedures for logging onto the system.

User Training Feedback

Telephone surveys the day following each session produced positive feedback and confirmation of the appropriateness of the two-hour training session. Arrangements were made with several engineers for advanced instruction.

The entire division was given an opportunity to be trained; over 90% participated in the classes. Although attendance was largely the result of management encouragement, the engineers found the time well spent.

Classes were held in the spring of 1983; a random survey taken in the last quarter of 1983 found 63% of the engineers still searching. Most individual search sessions last five to ten minutes, and the results are relevant to the inquiry. REIS found that the other engineers were using alternate retrieval methods. They either were using the indexes or having an REIS information intermediary do online searches for them.

CONCLUSION

This end-user project was really part of a larger program for making information—particularly proprietary information—more accessible to the end user. It is important to note that this is a complex goal that cannot be achieved only by a computer. We are convinced that the computer alone will never be the complete solution to the accessibility problem. End-user online access and training is a part of this solution, but we feel that other elements are just as important, especially a local document collection and a knowledgeable information intermediary assigned to the division. We feel it is also very important to continue to follow through and support such a project. Many projects with significant results in initial success have later withered because of neglect.

The success of this project was due to many factors. First of all, having information systems in place that could be utilized and skilled information professionals to work on the project were essential. REIS was in a position to respond to the division's needs utilizing full and skilled resources. The division management's support and direct involvement of the liaison engineer and the other engineers in the division were also essential.

The time spent analyzing the project, building the system, and preparing the training sessions and materials were crucial. The customization or individualization involved was also significant. The system, training sessions, and customized searching aids were all specifically tailored to the division's needs. REIS found physical proximity—the fact that the system, database, documents and intermediary, are physically located within a division—a very significant factor in the use of information resources. In particular, having a local information contact is an invaluable resource.

The whole project provided a good opportunity to expose engineers to the information management systems, databases, and other resources available at Exxon. A great deal was learned about the information needs of engineers, and they in turn have increased their understanding and awareness of us and our information services. The continued success of this project will depend on future interactions. The maximum utilization of information will occur with synergism—the cooperation of REIS staff and end users. It is to both groups' advantage to maximize this synergism.

REFERENCE NOTES

1. Walton, K. R.; Dedert, P. L. Experiences at Exxon training end-users to search technical databases online. *Online.* 7(5): p. 42-50; 1983 September.
2. Landsberg, M. K.; Lorenz, P. A.; Lawrence, B.; Meadow, C. T.; Hewett, T. T. A joint industrial-academic experiment—an evaluation of the IIDA system. *Proceedings of the 43rd ASIS annual meeting;* 1980 October 5-10; Anaheim, CA. White Plains, NY: Knowledge Industry Publications, Inc.; 1980; p. 406-408.
3. Landsberg, M. K.; Weil, B. H. Managing Exxon's technical reports. *Science & Technology Libraries.* 1(4): p. 55-64; 1982 Summer.

GOVERNMENT PUBLICATIONS REVIEW ANNOUNCES THE BERNARD M. FRY AWARD

Beginning with Volume 11 (1984) Pergamon Press is pleased to announce that a $500 cash award will be presented to the author of the best article to appear each year in *Government Publications Review*. The award will be presented in honor of the founding editor of the journal, Bernard M. Fry, and will be chosen by the *GPR* Editorial Board on the basis of cogency, style, and significance of contribution to the field of government information. The award will be announced at the general business meeting of the Government Documents Round Table at the annual American Library Association conference. For additional information contact: Steven D. Zink, Editor, *Government Publications Review*, University of Nevada Library, Reno, NV 89557-0044.

Teaching University Student End-Users about Online Searching

Sandra N. Ward
Laura M. Osegueda

ABSTRACT. An intermediate level of end-user education, between introductory demonstrations and complete end-user training, is defined and advocated. Several experiments in providing hands-on searching experiences for undergraduates and beginning graduate students at Stanford University and San Jose State University are described.

INTRODUCTION

This paper was written in an attempt to balance the literature on end-user training with consideration of an intermediate level of training: librarians teaching students just enough about online searching so that students can perform simple searches themselves and understand the nature of computerized literature searching. While the debate about end-user vs. mediated searches continues, we believe it is important to educate the students currently in our colleges and universities so that they will at least understand the options available.

The authors work in different institutions and hold different titles, but there is a common focus to our professional responsibilities and

---

Sandra N. Ward is Coordinator of Bibliographic Instruction, J. Henry Meyer Memorial Library, Stanford University, Stanford, CA 94305. She received an AB in Zoology from Mt. Holyoke College and her MLS from Columbia University.

Laura M. Osegueda is now Science Reference Librarian, D. H. Hill Library, North Carolina State University, Box 7111, Raleigh, NC 27695-7111. Until February 1984, she was Online Search Services Program Head, San Jose State University, San Jose, CA. She received a BS in Biological Sciences from the California State University at Hayward and her MLIS from the University of California at Berkeley.

interests. We are both responsible for collection development in science and technology to support undergraduate programs. We provide reference service to undergraduates in general and are actively involved in bibliographic instruction. We are also enthusiastic advocates of computer applications in libraries, such as online catalogs and computerized literature searching. It was therefore natural for each of us to seek ways to teach science students about online searching.

With the advent of end-user packages such as BRS AFTER DARK, KNOWLEDGE INDEX, SCIMATE, and SEARCH HELPER and with the proliferation of microcomputers, the idea of teaching students to do their own searching developed. We have considered many possible options ranging from brief mentions in existing bibliographic instruction sessions to full courses designed to train end-users. After much thought and some experimentation, we have evolved an approach to teaching ABOUT online searching in a way that involves students more actively than mere online demonstrations, yet stops short of full end-user training. Our interest is in incorporating this instruction into regular university courses.

We have found some examples in the literature of end-user training incorporated into university courses. Some interesting science examples include:

1. Teaching engineering undergraduates at Chalmers University of Technology (Sweden) to search BYGGDOK.[1]
2. Training chemistry students at the University of Cincinnati to search CA Search, MEDLINE and TOXLINE.[2]
3. Teaching biology students at Oregon State University to search BIOSIS.[3]

It seems that the objective of such instruction is to produce independent end-users. Specific databases and search systems are emphasized. Our objectives differ in the following ways:

1. Producing self-sufficient end-users is not our goal.
2. We are teaching ABOUT online searching in general, with emphasis on the process and strategy rather than the specifics.
3. Specific databases are used as representative examples only, with no expectation that the students will need to use them in the future.

4. We are using the online training as a "carrot" to attract student attention to reference tools and research strategies in general.
5. We intend to transfer the instruction modules into additional courses, changing subject examples and databases, as appropriate to the course content.

EXPERIENCES AT STANFORD UNIVERSITY

During 1983/84 Stanford students in several courses conducted their own DIALOG searches, supervised in a laboratory setting by librarians. A classroom equipped with microcomputers was used for hands-on searching labs, in which each student had an opportunity to spend about 20-25 minutes conducting online searches for subjects of his/her choice. This program developed from the conviction of staff in both the Stanford University Libraries and the campus computer center that students should be learning more about the capabilities of computers for information retrieval. The idea of a joint effort to teach "computer literacy" and effective library research skills emerged from talks between David Weber, Director of Stanford University Libraries, and Ed Shaw, Director of Information Technology Services (I.T.S.). The first author was assigned to work with an I.T.S. research assistant to develop specific proposals. Plans for an "information competency" laboratory that could be offered to (and adapted for) any Stanford course rapidly developed.

The first course for which the lab was planned was a proposed Fall 1983 course on ecology in the Program in Human Biology, an interdisciplinary undergraduate program that draws faculty from the biological, medical, and social sciences. Human Biology (HB) was considered an ideal test site because HB faculty were known to be supportive of both "computer literacy" and bibliographic instruction for their students. It was hoped that a successful pilot in HB would lead to rapid transfer of the idea to other Stanford departments from which HB faculty come.

During summer 1983 plans for the pilot lab changed abruptly with the resignation of the HB instructor with whom we had hoped to work. It was decided to work instead with the Fall Quarter section of *Library 1: Library Resources and Research Methods,* a 3-unit course taught by Meyer librarians and open to any Stanford student (undergraduate and graduate). Efforts to arrange a lab for future HB courses also continued. At the time of this writing (Jan. 1984), plans are well underway for incorporating hands-on searching labs into two HB courses in the coming months. These plans and the experiences with the Library 1 course will be described below.

Library 1: Library Resources and Research Methods

In Fall 1983 the students enrolled in Library 1 participated in two hands-on labs in which they experimented with searching several DIALOG databases. In the first lab, they searched PSYCINFO and SOCIAL SCISEARCH. Two weeks later, they searched MAGAZINE INDEX and other databases of their choice. Each lab ran for two hours, with four searching stations logged on continuously. The students worked in small groups, taking turns and advising each other, with librarians available nearby.

One interesting observation from the first hands-on lab was that all the students managed to retrieve some relevant citations (and to enjoy the process) whether they had prepared well in advance or not. Some of the students were very well prepared, with carefully written search strategies. They made excellent use of their online time and in some cases created large bibliographies. Others came with only vague ideas of their topics and the commands they should use. (It was deliberately left to the students to decide how much extra effort to put into preparing for the lab experience.) They learned by watching others and with coaching from others. All students learned that it pays to be familiar with the characteristics of the database to be searched. They also expressed a strong preference for databases such as PSYCINFO that have controlled vocabulary and a thesaurus that can be consulted in advance. The students emerged from the lab not only with printed lists of references on their subjects, but also with increased understanding of the power (and limitations) of computerized information retrieval systems.

Prior to the first lab, the students viewed a brief DIALOG videotape and attended a one-hour lecture/demonstration of PSYCINFO and SOCIAL SCISEARCH. Each student received the *Pocket Guide to DIALOG,* copies of the bluesheets for these databases, search strategy worksheets, and an assignment to select several topics for searching. One advantage of working with Library 1 students was that essential background information (e.g., about periodical indexes in general; about *Psychological Abstracts,*

Social Science Citation Index, and *Magazine Index* in particular; about controlled vs. uncontrolled vocabulary; etc.) had already been taught as part of the course. Even Boolean logic had been covered (for searching Stanford's new online catalog). The disadvantages included the lack of subject focus and the wide range of student levels (from freshman through postdoctoral). The lab seemed to be more successful the first time, when everyone experimented with the same two databases, than the second, when students chose a wide variety of databases.

The Library 1 labs demonstrated that undergraduates can, with minimal advanced training, successfully retrieve citations of interest to them from DIALOG databases. The students were highly enthusiastic about the process and eager for second and third turns. The Library 1 instructor was also pleased with the results. It has been decided to repeat the hands-on labs with slight modifications for the Winter Quarter section of Library 1.

Human Biology 112: Educational Policy

The instructor of HB 112 participated in the early planning meetings (Spring 1983) for the original HB "information competency" labs and observed one of the Library 1 labs with great interest. She requested that the same labs be repeated for her Senior Seminar on Educational Policy (HB 112) in Winter Quarter. Last year she required the HB 112 students to request online searches at the Education Library. She now plans to require the hands-on labs in place of the librarian-mediated searches because she believes the students will benefit more by learning about the online searching process than by receiving the higher quality bibliographies done by someone else. The Education librarian who conducted last year's searches and another social science reference librarian have been invited to assist with these labs.

Human Biology 40: Public Decision Making Regarding Human Health

In Spring Quarter 1984, selected students in *HB 40: Public Decision Making Regarding Human Health* will not only participate in the hands-on Dialog lab, but also will request (and participate in planning) librarian-mediated searches. HB 40 is an important policy course taught by a team of 10-15 faculty and taken by the majority of HB majors. Enrollment is expected to be 120-165 students—much too large for the present hands-on lab. Since HB 40 students work in teams of 3-4 students on a quarter-long research project and often divide the labor (e.g., one researches, one writes . . .), it has been decided to require that each team send one member for "information competency" training. This training will include emphasis on using the resources of the Government Document library and traditional reference tools as well as online searching. MEDLINE, SOCIAL SCISEARCH, and HEALTH PLANNING AND ADMINISTRATION will be searched in the hands-on labs. Three extra Teaching Assistants (TAs) will be hired to assist with this project. The Head TA will be invited to observe the Winter Quarter hands-on labs (HB 112 or Library 1) and then be sent to DIALOG for the 1 1/2 day System Seminar before taking an active part in planning how the hands-on labs will be integrated into the course schedule and assignments. Thanks to a grant from the Provost's Innovation Fund, each HB 40 team will also have a subsidy of about $25.00 for librarian-mediated searches if more comprehensive literature searches (or searches on different databases) are needed after the student hands-on labs.

EXPERIENCES AT SAN JOSE STATE UNIVERSITY

At San Jose State University students in several courses have participated actively in online searching. The instruction focused on database structure and online search strategies. Although the students did not actually input their own computer searches, they prepared the search strategies, observed the librarian-searcher closely, and advised her throughout the search. The classes included background information about periodical indexes, equivalent databases, their contents, structure and thesauri because we feel this material is essential when teaching students about online bibliographic searching.

These instruction sessions, which will be described more fully later, evolved naturally out of routine librarian-faculty contacts and the desire of the second author to gain experience in teaching end-users. In the light of impending library staff cuts and increasing student and faculty interest in doing online searches, the idea of creating a course to train library users to do their own computer searches developed. (For information about the planning for that course, see reference 4.) Active preparation for this course motivated the second author to explore alternative ways of teaching online systems.

As head of San Jose State University's Online Search Services, she received several faculty requests for online demonstrations tailored to the needs of their students. Some of these demonstrations developed into online training modules for courses in the departments of Biology, Music, Journalism, and Psychology. This paper will discuss the training sessions developed for students in Biology and Psychology. These lecture/lab sessions were held in the Online office used by librarians which is equipped with two online terminals. This facility was suitable because the class sizes ranged from sixteen to twenty students.

Biology 154: Computer Techniques in Biology

In Fall 1982, students enrolled in *Biology 154: Computer Techniques in Biology,* an upper division course, came to the library for two lecture/labs on computerized literature searching. The objective of these sessions was to teach these students enough about searching to provide an understanding of online search limitations and advantages, selection of search terms, and basic Boolean logic. A segment of the lecture described the computer hardware and software used in online searching. This tied the library sessions into the overall course content and took advantage of high student interest. BIOSIS was selected for the demonstration search because of its breadth of coverage. A large portion of the first session was devoted to explaining the use of the *BIOSIS Search Guide* and stressing its importance when developing search strategies.

After introducing the students to some of the basics of online searching, the class developed a search strategy related to their term project. This search was run as a class demonstration. The students were required to complete a search strategy for a BIOSIS search as a follow-up class assignment. The second session was used to assist the students with their individual assignments and clarify any questions.

Biology 154 was offered again in Fall 1983 and the online bibliographic searching module was repeated with several modifications. A demonstration search was run prior to the class and copies of this search served as the basis of the library/lab session. This proved useful to the students as an example from which to draw their own search strategies. Another modification was that only one library lecture/lab was necessary because the instructor had incorporated some material about online bibliographic searching into the course curriculum.

The modifications made during the second semester had both positive and negative outcomes. It was an improvement to begin the lecture/lab with each student having a sample search to follow during the lecture. This clarified how the computer searches for terms and combines them into sets. I was pleased that the instructor had felt that the computer literature searching component was important enough to be incorporated into his class lectures. However his students required more individual assistance before completing their assignments. An additional library session during the second semester would have allowed students to get help as a group, thus saving the librarian time in the long run.

Psychology 291: Methods and Design of Applied Research

Psychology 291 is a course designed to teach graduate Psychology students how to begin the search for their thesis projects. A new instructor in Fall 1983 added a personal file module to the course. He wanted to assist students in organizing their research material by allowing them access to an Apple computer in the Psychology department office. The second author was invited to instruct his class about indexing. It was decided to use established periodical indexes to teach indexing principles. *Psychological Abstracts* and *Index Medicus* were chosen because of relevant subject coverage, controlled vocabulary, and the availability of printed thesauri and online versions. Three class sessions devoted to library indexing and searching were planned. The initial objective of these sessions was to teach the students enough about online searching to perform simple searches and as a tool in developing computerized indexes in their research material. The hands-on component was continually postponed and eventually dropped from the sessions. It was the instructor's choice to have the students learn more about indexing and search strategies rather than DIALOG commands. Much time was spent discussing controlled vocabulary vs. free-text searching, various online strategies to keep searching flexible, ways to limit or broaden searches, and the online search strategies defined by Hawkins and Wagers.[5]

As each student was in the initial stages of writing thesis proposals and would be requesting an online search through the library's Online Search Service, examples relevant to their research were used throughout. As an outcome of their work in the course, the students developed their own computer search strategies which served as the basis for the searches run by the librarian. Even though the students did not actually learn DIALOG commands or input the searches, their active participation in the search process and increased understanding of computerized literature searching allowed them to feel "in control" of their computer searches. This team approach resulted in online searches that were highly satisfactory to the students, instructor, and the librarian.

SUMMARY OF EXPERIENCES AT BOTH INSTITUTIONS

These experiments at San Jose State and Stanford Universities evolved separately and were well underway when the authors met. We decided to write a joint paper describing a variety of means to accomplish the same objective, namely teaching college students about online searching. We want to stress the rationale for attempting this level of instruction and the benefits we have observed for students, librarians and educational programs.

Allowing students to become actively involved in the computer search process has the following benefits:

1. demystification of online searching
2. increased understanding of the search results
3. increased motivation to learn about literature searching tools and techniques in general
4. critical thinking about search strategy, choice of index, and evaluation of results

In our experience, students who have not had instruction in online searching and merely receive printed bibliographies from a librarian tend to attribute "magical" powers to the computer. They too often believe that the computer has searched all the literature and that the results are complete. They are unaware of the many possible choices involved in the process, such as selection of databases, keywords, and strategies. Without knowledge of what has been searched, they are unable to judge the results.

Students who have learned to prepare their own searches have a far better understanding of the complexities and limitations of computerized literature searching. They realize the trade-offs involved and are willing to try more than one approach. They are able to evaluate search techniques and results and have more realistic expectations of online searching.

A very valuable by-product of the students' active participation in computer searching was their increased awareness and motivation to learn about periodical indexes, subject indexing, thesauri, and the structure of the literature. In fact, both authors admit that our primary objective is to increase student proficiency in using library resources. We are using computer technology to attract the attention of both students and faculty; we are taking advantage of their high motivation to become "computer literate" and to save time in library research. This approach has been very successful.

IMPLEMENTATION AND FUNDING

We have learned from our experiences the importance of being flexible and open to opportunities for expanding library instruction on our individual campuses. Online labs such as those described above cannot be implemented without coordination with faculty and staff outside the library. This increases the complexity of planning the bibliographic instruction program, but also increases the options for sources of funds, equipment, facilities, and personnel.

The key to incorporating such online instruction into regular academic programs is adapting the instruction to meet the needs of the faculty and students. Specifics can be negotiated later, but the first step is to discuss possible options with interested faculty. Once faculty have become enthusiastic about involving their students in online searching, the focus of the instruction becomes clear and appropriate arrangements can be made.

Although the details will inevitably vary from campus to campus, and from one department to another within a given campus, a description of the arrangements made at Stanford and San Jose State illustrates some of the possible options.

Funding

The funding for the Stanford labs came from several sources. The discount rate available through the DIALOG Classroom Instruction Program (only $15.00/hour for a wide variety of databases) helped considerably. The Library 1 labs described above used about 16 hours of online time. The total cost including the initial demonstration was about $250.00. The Winter Quarter labs cost $160.00. The first author applied for a small grant from a library fund designated for innovative projects; the $860.00 received for the original pilot lab is now being used to cover both the Library 1 labs and a portion of the HB 40 costs. The Chairman of the Program in Human Biology applied for a larger grant ($4100) from the Provost's Innovation Fund to cover the cost of the extra TAs and the paid searches for the HB 40 course.

Before the HB 112 course could be added to the project, additional funding had to be arranged. Several possibilities including asking the students to pay for their own online time (which would be far cheaper than the searches they paid for last year) were considered. Since enrollment would be small, the HB Program agreed to cover the expenses ($115.00).

San Jose State University subsidizes part of the costs of computer searches for its students, faculty and staff. San Jose State University has made a commitment to have funds available for training and demonstration searches. This fund was sufficiently large to pay for the cost of the demonstration searches used for Biology 154. The average total for the BIOSIS searches was $30.00 each semester.

Costs of the searches for Psychology 291 were shared between the library and the Psychology department (through a grant held by the instructor). The cost of the first demonstration was only $11.87. Each student then paid for part of the out-of-pocket search costs for their individual research. The students' costs ranged from $15.00 to $70.00, with the library paying a maximum of $20.00 per search. The instructor used his grant money to assist several students with expensive and/or complex searches.

Facilities

Facilities used for the online sessions at Stanford and San Jose State Universities were quite different. The Stanford hands-on labs used the facilities and staff of the Stanford Microcomputer Instructional Laboratory Experiment, which was set up originally for a faculty "computer literacy" project. The S.M.I.L.E. lab is a classroom equipped with sixteen microcomputers, some with printers and all with dual disk drives. Monitors enable the students to view not only their own work, but also that of the instructor. Microcomputers were chosen rather than terminals because students are more likely to own or have access to them in the future. The students were also offered the opportunity to attend WORDSTAR classes in the same S.M.I.L.E. lab, so they could learn how to manipulate the bibliographies captured during the hands-on labs.

The San Jose State University library sessions used a less complex arrangement than Stanford's. Online terminals are located in several areas for library staff use: some in public service areas, some in private offices. The Hewlett Packard 2621P terminals used for the lecture/labs were convenient because they are equipped with both a built-in printer and a screen. Students were thus able to see the search as it was run. This illustrates the fact that no sophisticated lab set-up or equipment is necessary to teach college students about online searching. The only types of equipment needed are a computer terminal (or a microcomputer configured to serve as a terminal), a modem, and an outside telephone line.

Seizing Opportunities

The most important factor in implementing online instruction such as described in this paper is a willingness on the part of the librarian to seize opportunities that arise. Discovering even one faculty member, computer center administrator, or new microcomputer owner who is enthusiastic about end-user training can start the process. There is no one prescription for success. The first author became actively involved with Stanford's "computer literacy" planning after a casual cocktail party conversation with a key computer center administrator and was later able to link this general effort to the specific needs of the Human Biology faculty and students (for whom several bibliographic instruction sessions had been conducted in recent years). The online training sessions at San Jose State University developed naturally out of the library's regular online and bibliographic instruction programs. Both the Biology and Psychology departments had recently purchased microcomputers for departmental use. The Biology department was so interested in online searching that they obtained a DIALOG password and several faculty members have used this computer to do their own BIOSIS searches. This contributed to the interest to include computerized literature searching into a Biology course covering computer technology. The Psychology instructor was new to San Jose State University and had been a heavy user of DIALOG in the past. Through a reference interview a dialogue developed between the second author and the professor regarding his plans to use the departmental computer to set up personal files for new graduate students research. After further discussion it seemed logical for students to learn about indexing through the example of online bibliographic indexes.

Neither author set out in the beginning to implement the specific online labs described here. We simply believed that students ought to know more about computerized information retrieval and seized several opportunities along the way to accomplish that end.

Dealing with Murphy's Law

There are many variables involved in conducting online searches. Murphy's law indicates that the instructors of an online lab should be prepared to deal with any of the following complications: hardware failures, telephone or communication problems, system down time, and slow response time. For example, at Stanford the instructors learned one-half hour before the first lab that it would not be possible to connect more than two microcomputers simultaneously to TELENET (via Stanford's mainframe computer, to which all 16 microcomputers were linked). Two portable hard-copy terminals with acoustic couplers were quickly borrowed and set up with the S.M.I.L.E. lab's office telephones. This circumvented one problem, but raised two others: first, training students to use two quite different keyboards and later, coping with a sudden logoff when nearby telephone repairmen inadvertently cut one of the lines! In spite of these problems, the lab was considered highly successful by all involved.

At San Jose State, the second author was unable to access DIALOG due to system problems and had to use BRS for one lecture/lab session with the Psychology students. Students were still able to see the results of the search, but some additional instruction in interpreting the results was needed.

CONCLUSIONS

We are pleased with our experiments to date and intend to continue this intermediate level of instruction about online searching. We have demonstrated that undergraduates can, with minimal advanced training, become actively involved in formulating their own search strategies and conducting simple online searches. Online searching excites the students and motivates them to learn more about related reference tools and search strategies. After the sessions students have a greater awareness not only of the informational retrieval options available but also of the skills required by reference librarians who conduct searches for patrons. Whether the students will go on to become direct end-users or will rely on intermediaries for future searches is not important at this stage. The important point is that these students now know that they have such options.

We recommend that librarians in colleges and universities consider implementing such hands-on instruction for undergraduates and beginning graduate students, especially in science and technology because of the growing importance of online databases in those fields. We advocate an intermediate level of instruction between full-scale end-user training on the one hand and lecture/demonstration on the other. Providing students an opportunity to experiment with the actual process of preparing online searches, followed either by conducting the searches themselves or watching the librarian-searcher closely, is feasible and worthwhile. The details (whether to use terminals or microcomputers; in the library or elsewhere; Knowlege Index vs. regular DIALOG; etc.) are relatively unimportant and can be worked out in a variety of ways to suit local needs. The goal of the instruction in online searching is not to teach specific skills, which might become rusty or outdated, but to give students a basic understanding of the facts that these powerful online tools exist, that scientific and technical information is recorded and indexed in certain types of publications, that there are systematic methods (manual and online) to search for what you want, and that librarians can be very useful consultants in the process. The hands-on labs or exercises serve as excellent teaching devices to attract student attention and help them learn about the pros and cons of the online tools. If educated in this way, our students will be better prepared for future information retrieval challenges, whether in graduate school, in the business world, or in their personal lives.

REFERENCES

1. Fjallbrant, Nancy; Kihlen, Elisabeth; Malmgren, Margarita. End-user training in the use of a small Swedish database. *College & Research Libraries.* 4(2): 161-167; 1983 March.
2. Krueger, Geraldine L.; DesChene, Dorice. Introducing on-line information retrieval

to the undergraduate and graduate student in chemistry. *Journal of Chemical Education.* 57(6): 457; 1980 June.

3. Brooks, Kristina M. Non-mediated usage of online retrieval systems in an academic environment. *Proceedings of the 3rd National Online Meeting, 1982.* 35-39; 1982.

4. Osegueda, Laura M.; Reynolds, Judy. Introducing online into the university curriculum. *RQ.* 22(1): 10-11; 1982 Fall.

5. Hawkins, Donald T.; Wagers, Robert. Online bibliographic search strategy development. *Online.* 6(3): 12-19; 1982 May.

Managing Effective Information Services for End-Users in Academic Sci-Tech Libraries

Arleen N. Somerville

ABSTRACT. Effective information services support the mission of the university, increase productivity of the library's clientele, improve credibility of the library and librarian, and produce strong advocates of library priorities within the university community. Methods of identifying user groups are described, as are examples of user-oriented services (instructional programs, reference service, computer searching, current awareness services, provision of documents, photocopy services, intra-university delivery, and collection development). The importance of communication skills in achieving these objectives is emphasized. Such key factors as selection and training of staff and the importance of well-informed interactions with other library staff are discussed.

INTRODUCTION

Development of effective information services and a collection tailored to users' needs are primary objectives of forward-looking science and engineering libraries in academic institutions. Active and effective services geared to the clientele's needs benefit the university, the library, and the librarian.

Most importantly, such services further the university's mission of teaching and research, especially in the current competitive environment. Information services can increase the productivity and hence aid the careers of faculty, researchers, students, and administrators.

Satisfied users of library services become strong advocates for

---

Arleen N. Somerville is Head, Science and Engineering Libraries, University of Rochester, Rochester, NY 14627. She is also the chemistry, geology, and map librarian. She received the BS and MLS degrees from the University of Wisconsin.

© 1984 by The Haworth Press, Inc. All rights reserved.

library priorities and resources, an especially vital position in times of financial constraints. It is important for librarians to become so intimately involved and effective in recognizing and meeting users' needs that they achieve the status of "ingratiated irreplaceability"[1] in the eyes of their academic clientele. Such intelligent involvement in tailoring service programs to the clientele enhances the image and credibility of the library and the librarians, and enables users to view the librarian as a professional peer and as an irreplaceable contributor to their success as teachers, researchers, students, and administrators. Such a productive image helps justify professional salaries. In addition, jobs are a great deal more interesting and challenging when the savvy librarian exploits new sources, techniques, and technologies in providing a broad range of services. Provision of such services is not merely mechanical or procedural, but an attitude committed to an effective outreach program.

COMMUNICATION

Effective communication between library staff and all segments of the university community is the key to a successful information services program. Major elements in such a program include:

- —identifying specific information needs of each user group within the university community;
- —developing and maintaining services and collections that meet users' needs;
- —marketing services to each user group; raising users' consciousness about possible services;
- —following through on users' requests.

The accomplishment of these elements requires that librarians use effective communication skills. Discussions of library needs with users provide opportunities to market related library services, as well as providing information important for determining what library services and collections are needed. The process of answering questions provides knowledge of users' needs and is a way to inform users of additional sources and avenues available for answering their questions. In such ways, each element contributes to the accomplishment of the others, with the quality of communication determining the overall success.

MARKETING INFORMATION SERVICES

Marketing of services is an opportunity to sell yourself, your library and your services to your clientele. It requires that librarians be visible in the library and the academic departments. At the same time, it provides the opportunity to update your knowledge of teaching and research programs, changes in graduate and undergraduate curriculum, degree requirements, proposed programs, and faculty recruitment plans.

Each segment of the university community should be identified and marketing techniques targeted to each group. Although characteristics may vary between universities, academic institutions will generally include the following groups: faculty, full-time research staff, graduate and undergraduate students, academic departmental staff (administrative assistants, business managers, secretaries, shop technicians), and university administrators. Depending on the institution, alumni and personnel from local industries and research organizations may also be user groups.

Faculty and Full-Time Staff

Faculty members, with teaching, research and committee responsibilities, have a potentially wide range of information needs. They also constitute an important base of supporters and can be crucial allies in gaining support and resources from library and university administrators.

New Faculty

The arrival of new faculty offers opportunities to learn about libraries at their previous location, their research interests, and their teaching techniques, as well as establishing yourself as a professional who is interested in providing services and collections they need to succeed in their endeavors.

A letter sent to new faculty one-to-three months before they arrive helps establish such a tone and serves as an introduction, if you've not met them during their interview. Such a letter can include the following points: evaluation of the library's collections in their subject field; location of other university branch libraries (if appropriate) with relevant subject holdings; suggestion that they send information about the most important journals and books needed for their research and teaching, in order to have the titles on the shelves when they need them; and current policy for ordering new subscriptions (if appropriate). Propose that you visit their office after they've settled in to discuss their research topics and describe your library services. Additionally, provide your office location and phone number.

Follow up your letter with a phone call a few weeks after they arrive and schedule an appointment. Ask about their expectations of libraries, the special services of their previous librarians, and their initial experiences with your library. Discuss library services with examples relevant to his or her situation and procedures for book and journal ordering. Leave considerable time to discuss their research areas in some detail. In order for this exchange to be credible, you need to possess a basic understanding of the subject area. Explaining that your knowledge of their research subjects helps you select books and journals in anticipation of their needs prompts faculty to respond readily and comprehensively. Learning more about their research topics may trigger additional ideas for providing services. Depending on the library system, you may want to offer a free computer search.

Faculty

Once faculty are on the staff, contact should continue, in order for you to remain current with research topics, to remind faculty of current services, and to update them on library activities.

Ideally, visits in offices should occur at regular intervals, such as once every 2-3 years. This provides opportunities to update your knowledge of their research interests and of departmental activities, to review library services and collections, and to listen to their experiences using your library. Specific questions about turnaround time for their requests, responsiveness of staff to their questions, and availability of needed books and journals will solicit comments. Library usage patterns by their research groups and themselves are useful matters to discuss.

Informal settings offer some of the best opportunities for acquiring the most current information about departmental activities, curriculum changes, graduate student recruitment and retention, and research topics. Luncheon areas, especially those with lounges, and social gatherings, such as colloquia receptions and departmental get-togethers, offer other productive opportunities for discussion. An occasional short conversation in the library can be useful. Not to be overlooked is the walk between buildings, which can provide unexpected brief chats. Library newsletters, which may be appended to new acquisitions lists, can be valuable vehicles for describing library services, policies, and procedures. News notes can highlight new services and policies and describe library-wide activities relevant to the readers. Contributions to departmental newsletters are an alternative means for informing faculty.

Newly appointed department chairmen and library liaison representatives appreciate a visit from you, for it's an opportunity to discuss their roles and yours in their new assignment. It is usually important for these faculty to increase their knowledge of library procedures, budgeting, and upcoming activities as they affect their department. A review of the acquisitions budget process, how fund allocations are determined, the selection process, and factors to remember when monthly book fund statements are received, are typical topics to discuss. You should mention your role of interpreting the library to the department and the department to the library, as well as your responsibilities for ensuring that the collection is acquired to match faculty and student subject needs. In order to represent their needs, it's important to stress your need to stay current with such departmental plans as potential new faculty and their research subjects, anticipated new programs, and changes in enrollment levels. The importance of their advisory role should be discussed, along with recent examples. Ask to receive departmental mailings on a regular basis to ensure receipt of information, such as teaching and committee assignments, colloquia announcements, newsletters, receptions, and other social activities.

Meeting with research groups offers opportunities to reach a variety of users: faculty, research associates, post-doctoral fellows, graduate students, and upper level undergraduates. Discussions of information sources can be aimed at one or several related major reference sources, can focus on sources for a subject area such as biophysical or synthetic organic chemistry, or can introduce new sources. It is helpful to suggest alternative search techniques for typical questions. The same objectives are true in this more informal setting as for other information instruction groups: the researchers learn to select appropriate sources and use them efficiently.

All of this activity requires a great deal of time, so it is often wise initially to identify the most receptive, dynamic and influential faculty—the "gatekeepers."[2] These faculty will provide the greatest word-of-mouth publicity for your good work and hence contribute to your marketing efforts. In addition, they can provide you with information about the department, the subject, prominent researchers, and professional societies. Closer interaction can later be extended to other faculty as time permits and as consciousness is raised.

Students

Undergraduate and graduate students constitute a large percentage of a university library's clientele. As science students progress in their educational program, their library needs begin to match those of faculty and other researchers. During those classroom years, they require instruction in the use of information sources. The librarian's function is to provide the atmosphere and instructional programs that will produce graduates who can efficiently and effectively retrieve information and utilize library services.

Development of information instructional programs geared to students' needs is crucial for accomplishing such objectives. Additionally, contacts with undergraduate affiliates of professional societies (in such subject areas as biology, chemical engineering, chemistry, geology, mechanical engineering, and physics) offer opportunities to schedule brief talks beyond the instructional program. You may discuss such topics as typical lab situations in industry and how employees can effectively utilize the corporate library and its services. Student groups often suggest displays or collections of special interest to them (such as college catalogs). Members may also provide valuable comments about the kinds of questions they bring to the library—comments which help you to define the optimum service program and improve the responsiveness of reference service.

The arrival of new graduate students offers opportunities for small group tours of the library. In addition to the usual description of library layout, procedures, and policies, this time can be used to describe library services in some depth and to stress the staff's desire to help them find documents and information. A review of the location and value of major reference sources in their specialties may introduce students to these titles. In this way you establish yourself as a resource person who helps students in their courses and research work.

Department Staff

Close working relationships with secretaries, administrative assistants, business managers, and shop personnel facilitates effective communication between academic departments and the library. Good rapport can be important in accomplishing tasks such as setting up an accounting procedure or fixing a chair. These contacts are often excellent sources of information about departmental activities and can help you understand policies of the department. They can also ensure your receipt of departmental mailings.

The library can help them, too. Specially designed presentations for secretaries and administrative assistants can demonstrate the wide range of biographic, bibliographic and corporate sources available for answering questions that arise in their offices. Using specific questions can help bring home the point. For example, you may describe how biographic and bibliographic information helped a departmental nominee win an award, or how biographic and organizational data helped persuade a new corporate or government research sponsor.

University Administrators

Administrators include the decision-makers, (e.g., president and vice-presidents, provost and vice-provosts, and deans and assistant deans) as well as staff in other university departments (e.g., Development and Research Administration), who interact regularly with faculty and administrators. The first group, as the decision-makers, greatly influences resources allocated to the library. Therefore, it is important for them to see the library as an effective information service with a carefully selected collection and a university unit that is creatively using its resources to respond to faculty and student needs.

Developing a university administration supportive of the library requires that satisfied faculty and students express their approval to administrators. Conversely, requests for additional library resources are reinforced if faculty express the needs as well as library administrators. Faculty's promotion of the library's beneficial contributions to their efforts and their expression of unmet library needs can be effectively accomplished as individuals, as committees, as academic departments, or as task forces established for specific purposes. Librarians can directly influence deans' attitudes towards the library by meeting their particular needs, such as providing information for a speech or identifying subjects of general interest and forwarding selective items from current literature. Preliminary screening of information needed on a specific question is especially appreciated. Timely response to meet their busy schedule is crucial. Although presidents and provosts tend to have less need than faculty to use the library, all possible avenues for providing direct library support should be explored. Opportunities to give presentations about library services offer direct contacts for relating library services to their needs. For example, a library presentation on computer searching with examples keyed to their interests could be part of a university-wide review of computer resources. Through such formal means, as well as informal conversations, topics of interest can be identified. This could lead to the establishment of a highly selective current awareness service utilizing sources not commonly seen by the administrators.

Close working relationships between librarians and staff in Development and Research Administration can be mutually beneficial. Identification of their special interests can result in a much appreciated current awareness service. A current hot topic is industrial-university cooperation, and examples of successful programs are appreciated by Research Administration staff.

INFORMATION INSTRUCTIONAL PROGRAMS

Instructional programs which emphasize efficient use of information sources, search strategies, and the active role of librarians are the most effective means of student consciousness-raising.

Instruction plans for each discipline should be based on the unique information needs and use patterns of the subject area, and take into account the department's teaching objectives. (This assumes some basic library instruction is completed in the freshman year.) Extensive discussions with a variety of faculty, research staff, and students from each discipline are necessary to understand the curriculum and to plan the instructional program. The systematic introduction of information instruction into a variety of courses requires ideas and flexibility on everyone's part. Retention of an information course or addition of a course also requires extensive discussions and strong commitments by faculty and librarians. Exchanges with other subject librarians contribute also. These discussions may occur over several years, so it is wise to begin instructional activities with receptive faculty. This instruction, if done well, will enhance your credibility with faculty and increase your confidence. Each year's work builds on the previous year's efforts. Gradually an overall program can be built. Such a program should cover printed and computer sources, suggest optimum sources to answer typical users' questions (of that discipline), and ensure that students can select the most appropriate sources and can use them efficiently. The objective is to transform students into effective information users who see the librarian as a professional peer.

Consciousness-raising is equally important for research staff, including faculty, post-doctoral fellows, and research associates. Faculty who attend information instruction sessions with their classes update their knowledge of new sources and techniques. Ways of reaching other researchers include presentations as part of a regular departmental seminar series or discussions during research group meetings. Informal, one-to-one conversations often account for a large percentage of instruction for researchers.

Hand-outs and brochures commonly accompany information instruction and additionally support a wide variety of reader services. Publications may describe services by *type* (overviews, e.g., summary of information services, or specific, e.g., computer searching either overall or for specific subject areas) or by *location* (e.g., by library unit or group of similar units). Other handouts serve as guides to the literature. Here it is important to compile guides from the users' standpoint, which can be identified by talking with researchers. Such guides identify user questions typical of that discipline and suggest optimum sources to answer those questions. Depth of description for sources should reflect complexities of the materials and sophistication of the audience. Research-level users need guides which extensively describe use of the sophisticated sources.

INFORMATION PROGRAMS

An active marketing and consciousness-raising program must have a solid and useful product to sell. This requires development of a basic level of service attuned to user needs, which is expanded with increased understanding of user requirements. At the same time, services no longer used or needed should be eliminated. In such a way, a user-oriented library program can be built.

Reference Questions

Answering reference questions effectively is a basic component of such a program. Library staff who are approachable encourage questions from users. However, even the most friendly atmosphere will not prompt all users to ask questions. Staff need to watch for users who seem to be floundering and take the initiative to ask them, in a non-threatening manner, if they would like some help. Some users, especially at the research level, are unwilling to admit that they need help. For them it is more effective to ask if they have found *all* the information they need, or if the library has *all* the information they need. In this way, you avoid suggesting that they were unable to find any information. It can be beneficial to ask users, who are walking away from an abstract/index journal, if they found what they wanted and what subject they are working on. Their responses can prompt you to affirm the value of the index they used or to suggest additional sources. These extra efforts help the users feel that you are truly interested in helping them.

At all times the library staff must make users' questions *their* questions. This attitude requires that staff consider each question as if it is their personal question for which it is essential to get the best possible answer. Questions should be answered on a timely basis. However, completeness of answers should generally not be sacrificed for speed of response except under extraordinarily tight deadlines. All staff need to assume this strong service orientation before a successful information service can be achieved. Clerical assistants are particularly important, as they often work directly with faculty, staff, and students. Student assistants should be service-oriented as well.

A strong reference service answers a wide range of questions. Short answer questions such as decoding incomplete or inaccurate references, providing addresses of individuals and organizations, and identifying conference locations are staples in all libraries. Students and researchers are guided to optimum sources to answer their questions. Data are provided, such as density of a compound in liquid form. More extensive searches are done for faculty and administrators. Sources outside the library and the university should be utilized regularly as appropriate.

Computer Searching

Computer searching is now an integral part of reference service. It is used routinely for quick reference questions to save staff and user time. Access to a variety of systems is required to meet the needs of all science and engineering users. These systems usually include BRS, DIALOG, and SDC. Other systems that may be needed are CAS Online or DARC (for chemical substructure), SPIRES (for high energy physics), DOE or NASA Recon (for contractors with those agencies), ISI (for biomedicine, computers and mathematics, and geology), NEXIS INFOBANK, NIH/EPA Chemical Information System (for spectra, crystallography, environment, toxicology), and Infoline (plastics, paper, patents). Although use of multiple systems requires significant investments in on-going training and documentation maintenance, the wide range of information needs among users necessitates such efforts. The benefits of computer searching can be highlighted in talking with new faculty, researchers and graduate students, as well as with current faculty and students. Examples illustrating benefits and limitations of computer searching for specific subject areas of interest to an individual or research group may be especially productive. The opportunities for online SDI searches may also be discussed. Discussions associated with computer searches provide valuable opportunities for you to learn more about research projects and to review all sources available for the users.

Current Awareness Services

A service that supplies tables-of-contents of newly received journal issues helps researchers remain current in their fields. This is especially helpful to research groups with interdisciplinary subject interests or with laboratories and offices located a distance from the library building.

Informal forwarding of information to faculty and administrators on subjects known to interest them is much appreciated, especially from publications generally not seen by them. Faculty welcome information about commercial current awareness services, such as ASCA, ASCATOPICS, CA Selects, and CA/BA Selects. Benefits of scanning a *Current Contents* publication and opportunities for SDI computer searches should also be mentioned. Displays of newly received journal issues and books are popular ways for researchers to stay current in their fields. This variety of methods for remaining up-to-date should be covered in instruction sessions with students.

Provision of Documents

Science and engineering users often need documents quickly for reasons ranging from deciding what steps to take next in the lab to preparing grant proposals and refereeing those of others. Speed of delivery may be important enough to researchers that they are willing to pay for copies. It is crucial that science librarians recognize the need to acquire materials quickly, even if a cost is incurred.

Science librarians need to work in cooperation with the interlibrary loan department to provide documents quickly. Rapid verification of requests by science staff when sources are located in branch libraries reduces work for interlibrary loan staff and facilitates the processing. Discussions between interlibrary loan and science libraries staffs can promote understanding of each group's perspectives and can result in revised procedures that speed the processing at each step. Science staff should support library-wide efforts to decrease interlibrary loan turn-around time and encourage the library's participation in regional, state, and national network efforts to reduce delivery time.

In addition to using the interlibrary loan system, researchers appreciate the option of selecting a fast delivery method for a charge. These options include using document delivery services from database producers (e.g., Chemical Abstracts Service, Engineering Societies Library, Environment Information Center, and Institute for Scientific Information) and information brokers. Online ordering facilitates use of many of these services, although telephone and mail requests are accepted as well. Orders can be expedited as a "rush" request for an additional charge.

Photocopy Services

Photocopying articles for faculty is helpful in a number of ways. It provides a welcome service, increases the number of journal volumes available when needed because they are not checked out, reduces lines at photocopiers, and distributes copying over less busy times. Student help can copy the articles during those evening and weekend hours when copiers are in less demand. Photocopy service compliance with copyright guidelines should be practiced and made clear to the faculty.

Scientific researchers value highly ready access to photocopiers. Their need for specific information required in the laboratory often is found in a few articles which they want to copy immediately. Photocopiers located within a library and available whenever researchers have access to the library meet this need best. Additionally, accounting procedures that easily permit charges to research and departmental accounts are important.

Intra-University Delivery

Library systems with branch libraries rely on intra-university delivery of books, journals, and other materials between libraries. Those that provide delivery to faculty offices or departmental mail boxes find such service is popular.

COLLECTION DEVELOPMENT

A collection tailored to meet the clientele's needs is essential. Bibliographers' knowledge of users' interests will be comprehensive when they draw on experiences from information activities (e.g., reference queries, computer search questions) and from discussions with faculty and students. Likewise, their knowledge of selection decisions adds to reference service effectiveness.

Special emphasis should be placed on developing an effective working relationship with the collection development officer, as this person rarely has a science background. The officer should be kept up-to-date on curriculum and research changes (such as new programs, new faculty and changes in enrollments), which you learn about through conversations with faculty and departmental staff. Discussions about research patterns in science and engineering can provide the officer with a greater understanding of the differences between research in the sciences, social sciences and the humanities and the impact of on library needs. This information enables the officer to represent science areas effectively, as well as others, in library-wide discussions. Additionally, this information is important for allocation recommendations. Allocations, however, require specialized input from bibliographers, such as impact of series cancellations on monograph funds, significant increases in number of technical reports no longer provided free, and new major publications at high prices.

Discussions with acquisitions staff provide you with information about other aspects of the book and journal world and therefore widen the range of user questions you can answer. These opportunities to increase communication between the collection development officer and acquisitions staff and science librarians promote understanding of each other's perspectives and increase cooperation.

Close working relationships among the science bibliographers are vital, especially at universities with branch libraries. In those institutions, cooperation is needed to minimize unwanted duplication between libraries and to ensure that materials on a subject are housed in one location to the greatest extent possible. Because some duplication may be desirable, discussions with faculty and other researchers are necessary to identify those titles whose value justifies the cost of duplication. Especially careful monitoring of curriculum and research interests are required for such fast-growing and interdisciplinary topics as computers, robotics, cognitive science, optics, and energy. As applications and interrelationships spread into diverse subjects, location decisions become more complex. Collection development policy statements can provide structure for location decisions, when the policies are conscientiously updated.

STAFF

Selection and training of staff for an active information service program is crucial, because the staff's implementation of service defines the program's quality. All staff who interact with users must be service-oriented.

Librarians

Professional staff set the tone and provide guidance to other staff, so librarians should possess a strong commitment to active information service. A knowledge of science is essential for credible faculty discussions, in-depth reference and computer searching, rigorous information instruction, and accurate collection selection. Abilities to work effectively with a wide range of individuals and to manage time effectively are also crucial. Problem-solving skills are important, so librarians can implement effective user-oriented programs with limited resources.

With the changing worlds of subjects and technology, continual staff development is essential. Some of these needs can be filled by active participation in information and subject-related societies. Interaction with other librarians and attendance at technical sessions and continuing education courses can address many professional growth needs, e.g., management and supervision, new technologies, computer searching, and academic subjects. Activity in subject-related associations adds to professional growth and increases librarians' credibility with faculty, because they see you involved in activities similar to theirs. Programs within the university and library are necessary to supplement association activities.

Library Assistants

Ability to work effectively with many kinds of users is an important selection criteria for library assistants. Equally important is their desire to help people find what they need, and an eagerness to learn about new ways to help users.

Initial training should stress the importance of service and demonstrate how this is accomplished along with other assigned work. Ways of interacting with diverse types of users and of establishing environments that encourage users to ask questions should be discussed. Basic sources, techniques for answering typical questions, and question referral procedures can be ongoing topics for meetings and individual conversations. Library assistants also need training in new technologies and, if they supervise students, in supervisory skills. Library-wide and library department, as well as university, programs should address these needs.

Student Assistants

As an important, if not only, staff member on duty evenings and weekends, student assistants play an important role in implementing a service-oriented information program. Even during the day when full-time staff are on duty, students are often the first person users encounter. The quality of students' interactions with users should meet the library's standard. Training programs should stress the service and public relations aspect of the job, provide basic skills for answering typical questions, and teach the procedures required for the job.

Other Library Staff

Communication between science staff and other library staff is always important, but especially so when science libraries are located outside the main library building. Extra efforts are required to overcome the easily developed isolation, so science librarians should encourage opportunities for interaction with main library units. This can be accomplished by scheduling discussions of common concerns between science and non-science units and with staff exchange programs. Supervisors should regularly interpret other library units' pressures and priorities to help their staff see issues from all perspectives. Library-wide programs can feature faculty discussions about research and teaching methods common to their disciplines and how these unique, subject-related characteristics influence their library priorities and needs. Such programs can enlighten both library staff and participating faculty. Science staff should participate actively in library-wide committees and other activities to broaden their understanding of the library system, so they can respond from the overall library perspective as well as represent the needs and priorities of their constituents. These efforts promote greater understanding between science and other library staff, help create a more cooperative problem-solving environment, and facilitate library decisions that incorporate science community's needs as well as those of the non-science clientele.

REFERENCES

1. White, Herbert S. Organizational placement of the industrial special library: its relationship to success and survival. *Special Libraries.* 64(3): 141-144; 1973 March.
2. Allen, Thomas J. Organizational aspects of information flow in technology. *Association of Special Libraries and Information Bureaux Proceedings.* 20(11): 433-454; 1968 November.

American Petroleum Institute's Machine-Aided Indexing and Searching Project

E. H. Brenner
J. H. Lucey
C. L. Martinez
Adel Meleka

ABSTRACT. Because of the high cost of controlled indexing of bibliographic information, the American Petroleum Institute's Central Abstracting and Indexing Service (CAIS) has designed an expert-like system to take advantage of the 20 years of experienced indexing using keywords from its Thesaurus. It is expected that successful development of the automated indexing system could lead to a friendly system for the ultimate end-user utilizing controlled keywords.

In the development stage, the natural language keywords of the abstracts of papers are compared with the keywords chosen by the indexers and rules for cross references are added to improve the machine indexing. Noise is eliminated by additional rules. The system is designed so that the computer will convert words in an abstract to controlled keywords of the Thesaurus to such an accurate extent that the output need only be edited in order to achieve the quality of manual indexing. It is hoped that a user's query words may then also be converted to controlled keywords of the Thesaurus so that search strategies of the ultimate end-users can be enhanced.

INTRODUCTION

Retrieval systems have never been used well by most end-users. By end-users is meant the ultimate users who have the questions, who have need for bibliographic information and who will hopefully

---

E. H. Brenner is Manager, Central Abstracting and Indexing Service, American Petroleum Institute, 156 William Street, New York, New York 10038. J. H. Lucey is Systems Analyst, American Petroleum Institute. C. L. Martinez is Database/Education Specialist, American Petroleum Institute. Adel Meleka is Programmer/Analyst, American Petroleum Institute.

© 1984 by The Haworth Press, Inc. All rights reserved.

pay for information. Intermediaries, who have studied the great variety of input vocabularies and now can best take advantage of the technology of the computer, do the best searching, particularly if the end-user is readily available during the search. To let the end-users loose on our present systems except for simple searching would be a regressive step. They would search badly. They have always searched badly, even when they searched manually. If we truly wish to continue and even improve the quality of our searching, if we accept that end-users will never spend the time to educate themselves to present input systems, and if we no longer can afford the high expenses of intermediaries and professional indexing, we are then propelled into a future with a new approach to retrieval systems.

The catchwords of today, for the future in our field, are expert systems, artificial intelligence, and automatic indexing. The Central Abstracting and Indexing Service of the American Petroleum Institute has embarked on an expert-like system which could be of enormous help to intermediaries and could lead to good searching by end-users for even complicated questions.

THE PLAN

"An expert system can be thought of as an automated consultant. Operating from knowledge engineered into it by human experts, the system interacts with the users to solve problems." *(Monitor.* Sept. 1982, pp. 4-8 and October 1982 pp. 3-5). API's expert system (machine-aided indexing system) had been designed to take advantage of the 20 years of development work in the API Thesaurus and the 20 years of fully edited indexing. Thus, 20 years of expertly indexed documents have already been recorded. This expertise is being compared to the natural language of the abstracts that were actually used in the indexing process. A 40% exact match of natural language and thesaurus terms has already been found and it is hoped that an 80% match can be reached by applying expert system rules. If achieved, a controlled thesaurus vocabulary will be generated from the abstract and only editing will be required to duplicate or even improve on manual indexing. One could then project that an end-user could develop statements to describe his/her search. The vocabulary of the statement would be automatically converted to the thesaurus vocabulary and simple editing could produce an expert search strategy.

THE MACHINE-AIDED INDEXING PROJECT: DESCRIPTION AND CURRENT STATUS

Initially, a program reads the API Thesaurus to build a knowledge base. This knowledge base is then used by a program which compares phrases and words from the API abstracts to the phrases in the knowledge base. When a match is found, indexing terms are selected for the document.

Figure 1 is an example of the knowledge base from part of page 1 of the API Thesaurus. The first TEXT is "Abandonment" and it is followed by the term to use if the text is matched. In this case the text and term are the same.

The text "abrasion" on line 16 is derived from a cross reference so that the term used if the text is matched is not the same as the text.

The text on line 28 "ABS COPOLYMER" will result in four terms added to a document if it is matched.

The selection of phrases from the abstract for matching with the TEXT'S in the knowledge base starts at the beginning of the abstract (including the title). The first phrase selected is the length of the longest TEXT in the knowledge base. No stop word list is used.

If no match is found to the first phrase, it is altered in several ways and compared again to the knowledge base after each alteration. A sample of the original phrase and the alterations in the order of use is as follows:

Phrase	*Alteration*
LONG-RANGE PREDICTIONS PROVIDE	Original phrase
LONG RANGE PREDICTIONS PROVIDE	Eliminate hyphens
LONG-RANGE PREDICTIONS PROVIDE	Eliminate S from end of last word
LONG RANGE PREDICTIONS PROVIDE	Eliminate S from end of last word and eliminate hyphens
LONG-RANGE PREDICTIONS	Eliminate last word
LONG RANGE PREDICTIONS	Eliminate hyphens

Phrase	Alteration
LONG-RANGE PREDICTION	Eliminate S from end of last word
LONG RANGE PREDICTION	Eliminate S from end of last word and eliminate hyphens

BINGO! The knowledge base contains:

TEXT: LONG RANGE PREDICTION

TERM: PREDICTION

So the term PREDICTION is selected for the document.

The next phrase selected for comparison to the knowledge base starts with the word following the end of the phrase previously matched. In our example above, "PROVIDE" would be the first word in the next phrase. If there was no match, the starting point is advanced just one word from the start of the previous phrase. For example: if the phrase was "WHEN THE ELECTRIC FACILITY IS" and there was no match, the next phrase could be "THE ELECTRIC FACILITY IS IN SERVICE."

The process advances through the entire abstract selecting terms. The selected terms are entered into the CAIS indexing production computer database record for the abstract so that the indexer will see them displayed on his indexing screen when he starts to index the abstract. The abstract is also printed for use by the indexer with the terms selected printed next to the line from which they were selected. (See Figure 2.)

Initially, this process produces only 40% of the terms which the CAIS indexer would have produced on his own. It also produces nearly as many unwanted terms (called noise terms).

By running the process on previously indexed abstracts, we are able to produce statistical data and samples of the terms missed and the noise. Figure 3 shows some of the data for the terms missed for the 1982 API Transportation and Storage abstracts. The terms are shown in order of the number of times missed.

By reviewing samples of the abstracts in which the terms are missed we can determine what changes are needed in the knowledge base. By concentrating our efforts on the most frequently missed terms, we can get the greatest result from the review process.

FIGURE 1. Knowledge Base as Derived from API Thesaurus

THESAURUS		KNOWLEDGE BASE
ABANDONMENT *(5819)*	0001	TEXT:ABANDONMENT
Added in 1982	0002	TERM:ABANDONMENT
UF: Well Abandonment 82 *plus* WELL	0003	——————————
	0004	TEXT:ABIETIC ACID
ABATEMENT	0005	TERM:ABIETIC ACID
see: CONTROL	0006	——————————
DAMPING	0007	TEXT:ABNORMALITY
DECELERATION	0008	TERM:ABNORMALITY
POLLUTION CONTROL	0009	——————————
PREVENTION	0010	TEXT:ABOVE
SHRINKAGE	0011	TERM:ABOVE
	0012	——————————
ABIETIC ACID *(301)*	0013	TEXT:ABOVE GROUND
Index also C17-25 on the same link.	0014	TERM:GROUND LEVEL
Chem. Abstr. 514-10-3	0015	——————————
CA: SATURATED CHAIN	0016	TEXT:ABRASION
BRANCHED CHAIN	0017	TERM:WEAR
SATURATED CARBOCYCLIC	0018	——————————
UNSATURATED CARBOCYCLIC	0019	TEXT:ABRASION RESISTANCE
FUSED OR BRIDGED RING	0020	TERM:WEAR RESISTANCE
6 MEMBER RING	0021	——————————
MONOCARBOXYLIC ACID	0022	TEXT:ABRASIVE
MULTIOLEFINIC	0023	TERM:ABRASIVE
SA: ROSIN	0024	——————————
RESIN ACID	0025	TEXT:ABS (ALKYLBENZENESULFONATES)
ABLATION	0026	TERM:ALKYLBENZENESULFONATES
see: DETERIORATION	0027	——————————
EVAPORATION	0028	TEXT:ABS COPOLYMER
MELTING	0029	TERM:ACRYLONITRILE COPOLYMER
VAPORIZATION	0030	TERM:1,3-BUTADIENE COPOLYMER
WEAR	0031	TERM:STYRENE COPOLYMER
	0032	TERM:TERPOLYMER
ABNORMALITY *(1501)*	0033	——————————

Not for abnormality (operating condition), for which use OPERATIONAL PROBLEM.
SA: ACCURACY
UF: Deviation
    Erratic
    Unconventional

ABOVE *(1502)*
Modifier. Link to word modified. Added in 1966.
SA: OVERHEAD CUT
    UPWARD

ABOVE GROUND 66
  use: GROUND LEVEL

ABRASION
  use: WEAR

ABRASION RESISTANCE 80
  use: WEAR RESISTANCE

ABRASIVE *(1503)*
Material by function.
Added in 1967. Before 1967 search WEAR.
SA: SURFACE ROUGHNESS

ABS (ALKYLBENZENESULFONATES)
  use: ALKYLBENZENESULFONATES

ABS COPOLYMER
(Acrylonitrile Butadiene Styrene Copolymer)
  use: ACRYLONITRILE COPOLYMER,
    1,3-BUTADIENE COPOLYMER, STYRENE
    COPOLYMER, and TERPOLYMER, linked.

ABSENCE OF
(This is not an index term.)
For absence of a material, use NONE and the material, linked.

For absence of a property, use the property, e.g., for nonselectivity, use SELECTIVITY, unless an index term exists for the absence of the property, e.g., NONPOLAR, IMPERMEABLE, INERT. NONIONIC.

ABSORBANCE
  see: ABSORPTION
    OPTICAL DENSITY

ABSORBENCY
  see: ABSORPTION
    OPTICAL DENSITY

FIGURE 2. Abstract Printed for Indexer

```
TAN 201657            PAN 29-50304              Indexer        Editor


Pipe Line Ind. 56 #1:57-58,62(Jan. 1982)

FINAL APPROVAL OF AGREEMENT WILL CLEAR          CONTRACT
U.S.S.R.-[TO-WEST GERMANY GAS] LINE. Ruhrgas A.G.   WEST GERMANY
                                                NATURAL GAS
and Soyuzgazexsport have signed a natural gas   NATURAL GAS
import agreement. To implement the export       IMPORT
                                                CONTRACT
                                                EXPORT

program, which is still subject to approvals, the
Soviet Union will construct a $10-$12 billion   RUSSIA
                                                INVESTMENT
                                                COST
(U.S.), 3417 mi, 56 in. natural gas system,     NATURAL GAS
starting in the Urengoy field in West Siberia and  OIL AND GAS FIELDS
ending at the West German border. The system,
which will start construction in 1982 and be
completed by 1984, will be operated at 1087 psi.
Initially, 41 compressor stations, equipped with   PUMP STATION
gas turbine prime movers and centrifugal        GAS TURBINE
compressor driven units, will be installed. As  CENTRIFUGAL COMPRESSOR
natural gas production in the Urengoy field is  NATURAL GAS
                                                OIL AND GAS FIELDS
stepped up, the system will be extended to the as
yet undeveloped Yamburg field. Russia plans to tie  OIL AND GAS FIELDS
the natural gas field in the Yamal penninsula   OIL AND GAS FIELDS
into the transmission system at a later date.   PIPELINE
Russian authorities are considering extruded
polyethylene coating and polyethylene tapes for
corrosion protection. Construction will include CORROSION
manual stick electrode and MIG welding processes,  MANUAL
                                                ELECTRODE
                                                WELDING
and the Sever-I electric contact process welding  WELDING
system developed by the Soviet Union to weld    RUSSIA
                                                WELDING
large-diameter pipeline under the most severe   LARGE DIAMETER
                                                PIPELINE
climate conditions. Map.
```

The review process produces many new rules which are more complex than the simple TEXT and TERM match derived from the API Thesaurus. For example:

    TEXT: INSULATION
    SECT: LIQUIFIED GASES
    TERM: THERMAL INSULATION

FIGURE 3. Statistics on Terms Missed

	MISSES	TERM
1	481	CARGO
2	246	COMMERCIAL
3	229	CRUDE OIL
4	220	MEETING PAPER
5	220	TRUNK PIPELINE
6	182	REVIEW
7	166	CONSTRUCTION MATERIAL
8	160	NATURAL GAS
9	149	SPECIFICATION
10	128	TRANSPORTATION
11	126	EQUIPMENT TESTING
12	104	COATING MATERIAL
13	104	UNDERWATER
14	100	MAINTENANCE
15	97	PREVENTION
16	94	LINE PIPE
17	88	CONSTRUCTION
18	87	LEGAL CONSIDERATION
19	86	OIL AND GAS FIELDS
20	86	SUPPLY
21	84	INVESTMENT
22	84	PROCESS CONTROL
23	83	USA
24	78	GOVERNMENT
25	74	PATH
26	71	ACCURACY
27	70	PREDICTION
28	69	COST
29	67	PETROLEUM FRACTION
30	62	DOCK
31	62	NEWS
32	59	FLUID FLOW
33	59	INSPECTING
34	59	WELDING
35	57	DATA
36	57	ORGANIZATION
37	56	PERSONNEL
38	55	DESIGN
39	55	PIPELINE
40	55	REFRIGERATED TANKER
41	54	COMPOUNDS
42	54	MATHEMATICS
43	54	PLANNING
44	53	OFFSHORE
45	53	THROUGHPUT
46	52	SAFETY
47	51	CAPACITY
48	49	COST REDUCTION
49	48	STANDARDIZATION
50	47	COATING PROCESS
51	47	HAZARD
52	47	SOIL (EARTH)

FIGURE 3 (continued)

53	46	COMPARISON
54	46	MODIFICATION
55	44	EQUIPMENT
56	43	MAP
57	43	NATIONAL
58	42	DIAMETER
59	42	OFFSHORE STRUCTURE
60	42	OPERATIONAL PROBLEM

This rule says that when the text "INSULATION" is found in an abstract published in the LIQUIFIED GASES section of the API abstract bulletin, the term "THERMAL INSULATION" should be put in the index.

Many types of conditional relations are used in making new rules. So far, we have:

SECT: limit rule to a given section
SENS: apply rules only if another word or phrase is found in the same sentence.
DOCU: apply rule only if another word or phrase is found in the same abstract
COND: apply rule only if one of several conditions are met
ELSE: if the preceding set of conditions were not met, then consider the following
ALSO: after applying the previous set of conditions then also apply the following set

Here are some samples showing some of these conditional relations in use:

TEXT: FIRE

SECT: SAFETY

TERM: ACCIDENTAL FIRE

ALSO:

SENS: DETECTION

TERM: ALARM

TERM: ACCIDENTAL FIRE

ALSO:

SENS: EXTINGUISHING
TERM: FIRE FIGHTING
ALSO:
SENS: EXPLOSION
TERM: ACCIDENTAL FIRE
ALSO:
SENS: PREVENTING
TERM: SAFETY
TERM: ACCIDENTAL FIRE
TERM: PREVENTION
TEXT: DISCUSSION
COND: IN FIRST 2 SENTENCES
TERM: REVIEW

Current Status

Our first review process covered a 10% sample of the first 45 terms most frequently missed and the first 45 terms most frequently appearing as noise. The total review effort took about 5 man days. Applying the rules generated in this review provided an additional 4% of the terms the indexer would have entered. The noise was cut from 38% to 22%.

We are now in the process of doing a more detailed review of the first 100 terms in each category. This review required about 6 man weeks. After several more reviews, we expect to achieve about 80% of the terms with low noise.

MACHINE-AIDED SEARCHING: A PROPOSAL

The basic concept of this system is to have the microcomputer read natural language search queries and use the knowledge base being developed for Machine Aided Indexing to produce index terms for searching. However, the following description of the search utility is based on the API Thesaurus not on the knowledge base which is still being developed.

Search Utility

The hardware for this system would be a microcomputer with at least ten million characters of disk storage. The API Thesaurus would be stored on the disk with a set of indexes for fast access by computer programs.

The programming for the microcomputer would provide for accessing the API files on SDC's ORBIT system and for accessing the API Thesaurus on the disk.

The search query would be entered on the microcomputer prior to connecting the database. The microcomputer would match the phrases and words in the query to the Thesaurus and thus find search terms. For example, consider the search question:

EPA RULINGS ON THE LEAD CONTENT OF GASOLINE

A computer comparison of the words in the text to the API Thesaurus gives the following matches of Index Terms and Cross References:

Text	Index Term or Cross Reference
EPA	Use: ENVIRONMENTAL PROTECTION AGENCY
RULINGS	———
LEAD	LEAD
CONTENT	See: Composition
	Quality
GASOLINE	See: AVIATION GASOLINE
	GASOLINE STOCK
	GELLED GASOLINE
	MOTOR GASOLINE
	NAPHTHA
	NATURAL GASOLINE
	POLYMER GASOLINE

The words ON, THE, and OF would be removed by applying a stop list. The word RULINGS would be tried in the singular form

(RULING) after no match was found in the plural form. No match would be found to RULING also, but in the API Thesaurus, there is a cross reference: RULING, LEGAL use LEGAL CONSIDERATION. The microcomputer could be programmed to recognize the partial match up to the comma and to ask the user a question in such cases. For example:

BY RULINGS DO YOU MEAN: RULING, LEGAL?

ANSWER "YES" OR "NO" OR "EXPAND" FOR MORE DETAILS.

The user could then accept RULING, LEGAL by answering YES or see the Thesaurus entry by entering EXPAND. (In this case, the entry does not add any more information.) A response of NO would result in another question asking for a synonym. The user could supply one or direct the computer to drop the word RULINGS from consideration.

The other terms and cross references could be handled entirely by the computer for the end-user while options could be provided to allow more user interaction in selecting index terms by the trained intermediary. With no user interaction, the search strategy would be as follows:

TERMS TO BE SEARCHED	*(ORIGIN)*
1. U.S. ENVIRONMENTAL PROTECTION AGENCY	(EPA)

and

2. LEGAL CONSIDERATION	(RULINGS)

and

3. LEAD	(LEAD)

and

4a. COMPOSITION OR 4b. QUANTITY	(CONTENT)

and

5a. AVIATION GASOLINE OF 5b. GASOLINE STOCK OR 5 GELLED GASOLINE OR 5d. MOTOR GASOLINE OR 5e.

NAPHTHA OR 5f. NATURAL GASOLINE OR 5g. POLYMER GASOLINE   (GASOLINE)

Items 4 and 5 in the strategy consist of several terms connected by OR. These are derived from Thesaurus entries which direct the users to "see" several other entries.

By taking these "see" terms in an OR group, we avoid having to ask the users to make a decision.

If the user had opted for more interaction, items 4 and 5 in the above search strategy might be simplified by asking the user to pick one or several of the terms. Such interaction might occur as follows:

BY GASOLINE DO YOU MEAN SOME OF THE FOLLOWING:

1. AVIATION GASOLINE

2. GASOLINE STOCK

3. MOTOR GASOLINE

4. NAPHTHA

5. NATURAL GASOLINE

6. POLYMER GASOLINE

ENTER NUMBER AND QUESTION MARK FOR AMPLIFICATION OR ENTER NUMBER AND D TO DELETE FROM CONSIDERATION OR ENTER NUMBER AND S TO SAVE. (IF YOU USE S, ONLY THE ITEMS YOU ENTER WILL BE SAVED.) ENTER OK WHEN READY TO PROCEED.

)5?

NATURAL GASOLINE

Material by composition.

For a more complete search, search also PETROLEUM.

See also: NATURAL GAS LIQUIDS

          NATURAL GASOLINE PLANT

          -NATURAL GAS, NAT. GASOL., LPG

Used for: Casinghead Gas Condensate

          Casinghead Gasoline

                    Condensate (Casinghead Gas)

                    Condensate

                    Gas Condensate (Natural Gasoline)
)5d
5. NATURAL GASOLINE DELETED
)4D
4. NAPHTHA DELETED
)6D
6. POLYMER GASOLINE DELETED
)OK

A similar process could be used when a term selected from the match to the natural language of the query has "see also" directions in its Thesaurus entry. In this case, the user could select the original term as well as one of the "see also" terms.

The choice between these different approaches would be made by the user when the system is first started.

We tested this proposed search utility by randomly selecting four API abstracts published in 1982 and using the titles of these abstracts as search questions. We then manually went through the process of imitating the proposed search utility generating the search strategies. In working out the strategies, it was assumed that the person asking the question was not a trained searcher but an end-user who was not familiar with searching or API's Thesaurus.

Each strategy was then entered on ORBIT to search APILIT. The search was limited to 1982 to simplify evaluation of the results. A very experienced searcher of APILIT took the same questions and devised her own strategies. Her results were used as the standard against which the results from the search utility were measured.

The input queries were as follows:

1. Preventing Rust in Storage Tanks.
2. Economical Coal Liquefaction Processes.
3. Simulation of Detergent Flooding in a Vertical Cross Section.
4. Flame Blowoff Studies Using Large-Scale Flameholders.

A comparison of the search utility to the experienced searcher results as follows:

Query	Good Answers	False Drops	Missed
1	6	1	1
2	27	25	20
3	0	0	1
4	1	0	1

For questions 1, 2, and 4, the search utility provides reasonable results considering that practically no effort was expended by the user in devising the strategy.

In question 3, the problems encountered seem to be that the search query is too narrow and that the vocabulary as defined by the API Thesaurus is sometimes not adequate for the natural language queries.

With regard to the problem of the queries being too narrow, a trained intermediary could probably easily improve the strategies by changing some of the AND's to OR's.

If all of the AND's were changed to OR's and some kind of weighting and sorting were applied, the results would probably improve. However, since the search systems (ORBIT, DIALOG, and BRS) charge for each hit, this would be very expensive to run on the microcomputer. A typical search would involve tens of thousands of documents to be weighted and sorted.

The vocabulary problems will be greatly reduced by the application of the knowledge base being developed for Machine Aided Indexing.

SUMMARY

Machine-aided indexing based on the history of expert indexing built up over 20 years may save the high expense of professional indexing; A machine-aided search system capable of providing end-users with controlled vocabulary may lead to end-user searching without the loss of search expertise usually provided by intermediaries.

Preparation of a Slide/Tape Program for Biological Abstracts: Harvard University

Eva S. Jonas

ABSTRACT. Describes the techniques used by the author in preparing a slide/tape program for *Biological Abstracts* for use at Harvard University's Cabot Science Library.

INTRODUCTION

Cabot Science Library at Harvard University places great importance on the service provided undergraduate science students. It was noted that many undergraduates lacked skill in using important abstracting and indexing services, including *Biological Abstracts*. Accordingly in 1976 the author, as Reference Librarian having responsibility for bibliographic instruction in that library, saw the need for an aid for undergraduates wanting to use that indexing service. It was decided to produce a slide/tape program describing its features. *Biological Abstracts* is not a simple tool for the uninitiated to learn to use, and it was felt that this program would be well worth creating.

Consequently the first edition was prepared in 1976, with a revised edition prepared in 1981. It has subsequently proved to be well liked and has been used in library schools, medical training programs and sci-tech libraries all over the country. The project took one month of full commitment and later another forty hours before it could be published.

Eva S. Jonas is Librarian, Museum of Comparative Zoology Library, Harvard University, Cambridge, MA 02138. She was educated in general zoology and library science at Charles University in Prague; she later received an M.A. in developmental biology from Harvard University.

© 1984 by The Haworth Press, Inc. All rights reserved.

The remaining portion of this paper reflects the author's experience in the production of this audiovisual tool.

BACKGROUND

Slide/tape programs have become efficient tools used in bibliographic instruction programs in academic libraries. They can be used for group and classroom instruction as well as on an individual basis. Besides improving the quality of bibliographic instruction, they save time in the long run. They are also the best means of instruction in situations where a research library cannot afford skilled instructors on duty all the time. In that sense they replace a reference librarian in many ways. It is clear, however, that only *well produced* slide tapes can fill this need—especially those designed for instruction on the use of complex reference tools.

This article points out the most important aspects of slide/tape preparation for bibliographic instruction in the use of complex reference tools. It describes those aspects of slide/tape production which, in the author's view, differ from commercial and basic information slide tapes. In no way is this intended to be a complete recipe on how to make slide/tapes; it is designed to give "special" hints to supplement the published descriptions of slide/tape production.[1-3]

Before getting involved in any slide/tape preparation, the reference librarian should review existing tapes in the same or similar subjects and set clear guidelines for what the tape should cover and at what level. When preparing slide/tapes for academic use, one should avoid publicity and commercialization in the contents. For most academic users that information is unnecessary and uninteresting and reduces the attractiveness of the slide/tape. It adds time without adding instructional content.

STARTING WITH THE SCRIPT

The first step is an outline of the script. The first actual draft of the script should cover all information about the reference tool in a clear manner. The draft should be reviewed several times, and it should be reviewed by people other than the author for comments. The logical sequence should form the skeleton of the script. (At this point, scissors and tape for rearranging sentences are as essential as a pen. A word processor would be even better.) After the author is satisfied that the script covers the subject adequately and no logical link is missing in the narrative, the chapters of the script should be reviewed from a different angle. The author should select which parts of the instructional content should be covered by a slide, and which by accompanying narrative. It is wise to include all information likely to be changed on the slide since it is much easier to replace a slide in an updated version than to replace the narration. There is, of course, a limit to this, but good planning could save time in the future. The most difficult concepts and relations should be covered by "composite" slides, slides made up with clear examples, explanations, and footnotes.

Here lies the success and strength of this type of instructional material. Visual instruction accompanied, or even better, followed after a few seconds by a verbal explanation, works much better than a oral explanation (no matter how detailed) without a logically designed slide preceding it. The amount of "silent" time given for study of each slide before the narrative continues is crucial for a successful instruction. Contrary to publicity or orientation slide/tapes where the fast changing of slides seems to be a fashion, instructional tapes need pauses long enough for a user to digest all the information covered by the slide. A maximum amount of slides for a 20 minute instruction seems to be 60, allowing at least 20 seconds per slide on the average. The planning of pauses between slides is as important as planning their content and sequence. All this shows the importance of having as perfect a script as possible before any further work is designed. The exact moment for each slide to drop should be included as part of the script.

PRODUCTION OF SLIDES

It is helpful to have a folder with materials for each individual slide. In that way slides can be designed as "collages" from sample pages with appropriate highlighting. Colored transparent papers or special colored pencils can be used. There is a limit to how much each slide can cover—it is wise to make two or three single slides rather than accumulate too much information on one slide, thereby producing a "maze."

After all slides are designed, the narration should be matched with them again and revised for clarity. If everything seems to fit in place, the slides should be produced. It is wise to take two pictures of each slide and choose the better one. All original slide materials should stay in individual folders even then. Some slides may need reshooting at some future time if updating is needed. The photography should be done in as professional a way as possible.

TAPING THE NARRATION

Then comes the time for taping the instruction. Choosing a good narrator is very important. A monotonous voice will not work well; neither will one that is too exciting or nervous. The tape amplifies any excitement in the voice, especially at the beginning of the narration. Since virtually everybody gets nervous when he or she starts the recording, one can add two sentences at the beginning and cut them off later (or start the actual recording with the third sentence).

Three people are needed for a successful recording session. The first is the narrator, who should know the text very well and rehearse it with the author several times before the actual recording. The author would indicate to the narrator correct emphasis of the reading by raising or lowering the voice and by pauses. During recording the author should "conduct" the narrator at the beginning of each sentence for adequate pauses between sentences, many of which represent pauses designed for the viewer to read the slides. The author also monitors the correctness of the narration. The third person is the audio-visual technician who runs the audio workings and stops and restarts the tape when errors are made. It is important when portions are renarrated for him or her to leave a few seconds at the beginning and at the end to allow enough room for planned "silent time" after the tape is prepared. Then comes the cluing of the tape by signals for automatic slide viewers. This is also done by the author, who can best see that the right moment for each slide as determined by the script is chosen. The clues can be repeated and changed if not placed right at first.

REVIEWING

Now that the tape is ready to be tested, the typical users, students interested in the reference tool, make the best audience. Their comments should be followed—especially if they show that some parts of the tape need more explanation and clarity. It may be necessary to reshoot the slides and rewrite the tape. All this should be planned for from the beginning. If the time schedule and budget did not take this into account from the beginning, one would end up with an unfinished and certainly less useful product for any bibliographic instruction activity.

USE OF THE SLIDE/TAPE

The most difficult part of the job may actually start when the slide/tape is finished. It all depends on the level of acceptance of a bibliographic instruction program in the library and in the community which the library serves. It is naive to expect that many users will on their own seek out and/or use programs like this which involve equipment with which they are not familiar. Proper encouragement and help from the reference staff helps with the hesitant and shy patron. The reference staff has to work on publicity and find ways to reach users when their motivation is high. Some libraries organize an open house at the beginning of a school year and make an informal presentation of all the special services the library offers. Very often that triggers enough interest for people to come back, watch the tapes and spread the word. An even more effective way is to incorporate a certain segment of the tape into class instruction. Students are likely to be really interested in library research then, and if the segment of the tape is well chosen, they are likely to come back later and view the whole tape. The tape helps the librarian prepare for any class or group instruction concerning that subject. It also helps in training new staff. These are the areas where the library benefits most from a well produced tape. High quality instruction can be achieved without time-consuming, repetitious preparation for instruction and training.

REFERENCES

1. Association for Educational Communications and Technology. *Producing slide and tape presentations.* Washington, DC; 1980.
2. Kemp, Jerrold E. *Planning and producing audiovisual materials.* 4th ed. New York: Harper & Row; 1980.
3. Brown, James. W.; Lewis, Richard B.; Harcleroad, Fred F. *AV instruction: technology, media and methods.* 6th ed. New York: McGraw-Hill; 1983.

Increasing End-User Awareness of Library Services Through Promotion: Grumman Aerospace Corporation

Claude E. Gibson
Harold B. Smith

ABSTRACT. Awareness that usage of the Technical Information Center of Grumman Aerospace Corporation was not keeping pace with the increased capabilities provided by the Center led the managers of the unit to consider means for widening awareness of the services within the Company. A set of flip charts for use in presentations to those in engineering, marketing, research and product support/planning led to preparation of a slide/tape program, which in turn led to development of a video tape version. Some of the problems encountered in such activities are described, along with information on the type of equipment needed.

INTRODUCTION

Why promote end-user awareness of library services? Doesn't everyone who needs information know that the library or information center is the first place to contact? It is, in the opinion of the librarian or information specialist.

Unfortunately, for as many people who know enough to use

Claude E. Gibson is Deputy Director—Presentations Services, Grumman Aerospace Corporation, Bethpage, NY 11714. He has a BS in Chemistry from Rensselaer Polytechnic Institute, the MLS in Library Science from the University of Southern California, and the MBA from Adelphi University.

Harold B. Smith is Manager—Library and Information Services, Grumman Aerospace Corporation. He has a BA in Sociology from C. W. Post College, and the MLS in Library Science from Palmer Graduate Library School, Long Island University.

© 1984 by The Haworth Press, Inc. All rights reserved.

library resources, there is an equal number and more who do not. Their research technique is to rummage through desks or file cabinets for information. Or, they may call a colleague for suggestions or leads to "answer" questions. But does this approach produce a complete or comprehensive answer to questions? No!

The widely discussed information explosion is alive and kicking. It is unlikely that any single source will be sufficient to answer the compound questions which arise in today's business environment. As librarians, we know that the solution is to harvest many sources of information, review and weed out the chaff and provide factual information.

Our potential users, on the other hand, are not always aware of our capabilities. Some view the library as an archival storage facility, not as a dynamic research and investigative arm of whatever organization we represent. Many times this attitude on the part of both old and new employees is due to a lack of awareness that the library even exists, or that new services are available, or that existing capabilities have expanded.

Are there benefits to be derived from promoting library awareness? Yes! By better understanding and utilizing the capabilities of the library, the end-user will be able to spend more time fulfilling his or her primary function, analyzing and evaluating the research results with library personnel doing more of the research. The end-user has greater potential for higher productivity. No longer will the end-user be working in a vacuum with outdated or incomplete information.

There is also a benefit to the library itself. As management becomes aware of the resources available through the library, they become more receptive to supporting its needs. If we are to maintain and/or increase our information resources and capabilities, continuing management support is vital.

As information professionals, we keep abreast of the latest technologies and sources of information. We should not be afraid to change the methods or techniques by which we provide information. But are we always as dynamic in the way we promote or market our capabilities? Sometimes we get so wrapped up in increasing our capabilities that we forget to educate our users.

We are all aware to one degree or another of the more standard ways of promotion. Newsletters, acquisition bulletins, library handbooks and in-house newspaper articles are tried and true methods of library promotion.

PRODUCTION OF THE VIDEOTAPE

At Grumman we decided that in addition to some of the standard approaches we would also do something a little more dynamic, a videotape presentation. However, even this evolved from a basic flip chart presentation.

A rough draft of a flip chart presentation was created and turned over to the Grumman Presentations Services Department for editing and final preparation. The next step, always difficult, was to make the presentation to colleagues (other department heads) for critical review. It was at this point that a new dimension was suggested by the manager of Presentation Services; to add some photographs to illustrate some of the major points. It sounded like a good idea, so we had further discussions to explore the idea. We realized that photographs alone would present a problem by not being easily seen from a distance so we decided to go a step further by using projected color slides instead of prints. As we began to make a list of scenes to photograph and that list grew longer and longer (the original suggestion had been to use five or six pictures), someone suggested that we just tape the talk part of the presentation and then use the tape with the slides. In other words, make it a sound-slide presentation utilizing current A/V technology. Now we had to rethink our situation and decide if we really wanted to "get that fancy." Could we afford it? Our simple, relatively cheap flip chart presentation was evolving into a much less simple and quite a bit more costly effort. It was time to consider our overall long term objective and try to arrive at a conclusion as to the best and most cost effective way to achieve that objective. We wanted to address as many of our engineering, scientific, marketing and management personnel as possible. We envisioned a small group setting (no more than 30 to 40 people at a time). We wanted to stimulate interest in our services. The idea of a taped talk to provide a higher quality presentation was especially appealing. After weighing all the factors, and with the encouragement of our management, we decided on a sound-slide program with a professional reading the narration.

The next step was to develop a script to cover our objectives. For starters the original flip chart presentation was talked through and recorded on tape from which a typed transcription was produced.

By this time several weeks had elapsed and we were beginning to wonder if this promotional gem, which had appeared to be so simple and straightforward in the beginning, would ever get off the ground.

We were not terribly optimistic, a feeling magnified by the fact that we were dealing in areas somewhat alien and unfamiliar to us.

With the transcript in hand we proceeded to the next step, breaking the narration into single thought segments. This was done by placing a slash mark at the beginning and end of each thought segment. The material was then retyped on the right half of 8½ × 11 inch paper with each delineated segment numbered and separated from the next by several (five or six) lines. This was done to leave the left side of the paper to be used for picture notes (See Figure 1). This constituted the first rough draft of the script.

22. Close up of the output side of the press showing the printed material coming out, then cut to printing liaison specialist checking some of the previously seen material stacked up on the desk.

22. In spite of the volume of work and short turn around times, Presentations Services has never missed a deadline.

23. Med shot, editor at a desk in presentations department working on pile of roughs for art work.

23. The support of visual presentations is another large share of the departments work.

24. Med shot of some of the editor's roughs then cut to editor reviewing the roughs with requester as they are stuck on a cork board.

24. Visually oriented editors working closely with the requesters plan the material and get approval for the layout.

25. Editor talking to illustrator and with head of illustration dept. Cut to a shot showing PMS sheets with overlays scattered on top. (Need new slide as present slides over-emphasize Kodalith process.

25. Techniques for completing the final visual are determined in cooperation with the art department.

25A. Several slides of Genigraphics with image on screen.

25A. There are many techniques available, including a computer aided slide making system. Experience is required to pick the one that can accomplish the job effectively in the time available.

26. Designer working on board with a combination slide using art (that is a photograph or drawing) and laying curves over it. Cut to close up of the art itself. (Need new slide for same reason).

26. There are many paths to the same goal, effective, high impact visuals, but they all depend on the designer who does the final layout and designates the colors that will be reproduced.

27. Cut to vertical shot of the finished art and then match dissolve through the art to a complete color slide of the art.

27. And then through photography, black & white or colored art can be turned into full color visuals, ready for use.

FIGURE 1

After review by several people on the TIC staff, a revised draft was readied and turned over to an editor in the Grumman Presentations Services Department for further refinement and improvement. After further revision we were ready to begin specifying scenes to be photographed to go with each of the numbered paragraphs. A photographer, assigned by the Photo Services Department, accomplished the photography, using the script as his guide. Scenes included views of the interior of the TIC, staff members at work, arrangements of books, reports and magazines, patrons using the TIC, some examples of products whose development might have been aided by TIC support, etc. In all, several hundred pictures were taken to provide the selection needed to illustrate the script. Most of the script segments required more than one photo. No slide would be on screen for more than 5-10 seconds to maintain the pacing and rhythm of the program.

When the initial group of slides was selected, a rough version of the narration tape was created. This is called a "scratch track" and is used to match the slides to the script in order to visualize the pace and timing and/or need for more or less slides. Therefore, just as the script itself was edited and revised until a final draft was achieved, the slides to go with the script were also edited until we had the right mix and the timing was correct. In all, the final program was comprised of some 200 or so slides for a program that runs about 15 minutes.

By this time several months had gone by and our pessimism had gradually changed to cautious optimism. We could, at last, begin to see a product, albeit still rough, taking definite shape.

With the completion of the next step we felt like we had made the final turn and at last were in the home stretch. A professional narrator was retained to narrate the script. In our case the narrator was an announcer for a New York City radio station who had previously been used by the Company. It should be noted at this point that the professional narrator *must* be directed because his understanding of the program may differ from that of the creators of the program.

Next the narration was "clean cut" by a sound editor who cut out all but the good takes. It was also at this point that pauses were inserted as indicated. The final narration track was then played against the slides and a decision concerning type and placement of music was made.

At this point a few words of caution are in order. Music to be used must either be free of copyright restriction or, if protected by copyright, must be cleared for use with the holder of the copyright and appropriate royalty fees paid.

Once selected, the music is recorded by a sound or music editor on tape from discs that are commercially available. This person also is responsible for making sure that all license fees are paid and all clearances obtained. This editor then synchronizes the music and the narration track adding musical bridges at transition points and musical "stings" to make a point. Finally, the narration and music are mixed onto one track. We are now ready for programming.

Programming is a very sophisticated process requiring special skills and taste. The programmer plays the track back and forth and, using a computer, indicates the length of time each slide will remain on the screen, the length of dissolves between one slide and another, and makes adjustments as necessary to fit the narration and music. When the programmer has finished, the music, narration and projector cues are transferred to an audio cassette.

For our show three Kodak Ektagraphic slide projectors were used. Three projectors is the minimum number for a program of this nature although more may be used, i.e., 6, 9, 12 up to 18. It is thus self evident why the person doing the programming must have special talent and skill.

Once we were satisfied that everything was "just right" with the sound-slide show we moved on to the final step—videotaping. The transfer to video was done in "real time," i.e., a video camera was set and the show recorded as it was presented. You may use either front or rear projection for the show when doing the video recording.

When putting a show of this type together there are a number of potential problem areas or pitfalls to be avoided.

The script is the key element to the success of the whole program. Script design and writing require several inputs, and neglecting any one of them can lead to disaster.

A very important requirement for script preparation is to identify your primary audience by age, level of sophistication, knowledge of the subject matter covered, etc. You then need to determined what you want your audience to do after it has seen the program. These are very important behavioral considerations and should not be overlooked.

Another area to be wary of is the inclination to include too much information in a very detailed manner. In general, the audience will take impressions from the program but will not often remember discrete bits of information. While the use of discrete bits of information is perfectly acceptable to create an impression, don't expect the audience to retain more than the impression.

Another thing to keep in mind while reviewing the script is the natural inclination of people to "read" words rather than "hear" words. Words that are designed to be heard are strung together in a somewhat different form than words that are designed to be read. If the brain does not comprehend a phrase at first reading, the eyes will most likely receive a command to rescan it and, when it is understood, the eyes move on to the next phrase. The audience cannot "rescan." Once the words have been spoken, the program moves on. Therefore the meaning, heard only once, must be clear and emphatic.

The script must be complete and agreed on before any photography is begun as it provides the only guidance the photographer has to set up shots that will provide a cohesive and visually interesting program.

Don't skimp on slides. A good photographer will shoot 3-4 times as many slides as actually needed so as to provide a wide variety of choice, different angles, etc. for the programmer. The more slides you use the faster the program will move, maintaining greater visual interest.

One last problem to be aware of is that the picture format for slides has a height to width ratio of 2 to 3. The TV picture format has a ratio of 3 to 4 which means that if you intend to transfer the program to video some of the information from either end of the slide will be lost. If the photographer is aware of this, the important information, and this includes any titles, can be positioned in such a way as to avoid loss. Needless to say, all slides must be horizontal.

Next, a few words about cost. The least costly elements in putting a program like ours together are the film and tape (video and audio). The real cost is in the labor involved in script writing, photography and programming. The amount of labor involved is a function of the program's length and complexity, i.e., the use of more projectors will be more complex than the use of the basic three projector setup. While our production took the better part of a year to complete, it could probably have been done in a couple of weeks of concentrated time. The creative process doesn't work that way though and there are usually many other tasks in the jobstream at the same time. A reasonable estimate for a job of this magnitude would be in the area of about $5,000 in current dollars. This, of course, would depend on the overall overhead and benefit structure in any given situation. Keeping in mind the fact that we were trying to make our services more widely known so that we could better support the company's business seeking activities and improve the company's competitive posture, the investment was negligible.

EQUIPMENT NEEDED

In addition to the normal photographic apparatus needed such as a 35mm camera, appropriate lenses and lights, the following, more specialized, equipment is required for program production:

1 — High quality multi-track reel to reel tape recorder
1 — A/V computer programmer
1 — Turntable for playing purchased (and cleared) music discs
— Light tables for slide sorting
1 — Video camera and recorder for transfer of the completed program to videotape
1 — Cassette recorder.

The equipment listed is rather specialized, so unless there is a plan to produce many programs, the use of an outside producer might be more cost effective. Such speciality houses are listed under "Audio-Visual Productions" or some such a heading in the "Yellow Pages."

In order to show the program the following equipment is necessary:

3 — (minimum) Kodak Carousel projectors (or equivalent)
1 — Dissolve control unit
1 — A/V cassette playback unit.

Additionally you will need a videotape playback unit and a television set for viewing the completed videotaped version. With the above equipment the program may be presented in either sound-slide or television format.

Do the payoffs warrant the time and expense required to prepare such a promotional program? We believe they do. Access to information, in a comprehensive and timely fashion, is the key to staying competitive in today's marketplace, deciding to bid on new proposals, or to enter new markets. Increased productivity is still another facet.

The return on investment for library services is greater as more people avail themselves of the library services.

Promotion of library services is one way to increase their use. Increased use will guarantee a greater return on the investment necessary to provide those library services.

NEW REFERENCE WORKS IN SCIENCE AND TECHNOLOGY

Robert G. Krupp, Editor

Reviewers for this column are: Kathy L. Belyea (KLB), Technical Library, Bell Laboratories, Whippany, NJ; Carmela Carbone (CC), Engineering Societies Library, New York, NY; Robert G. Krupp (RGK), Maplewood, NJ; David A. Tyckoson (DAT), Iowa State University, Ames, IA; and Barbara Walcott (BW), Health Sciences Library, Columbia University, New York, NY.

EARTH SCIENCES

Carter, M. *Geotechnical engineering handbook.* Plymouth, England: Pentech Press Ltd.; 1983. 226p. $35.00. ISBN O-7273-0702-9. (U.S. distributor: Chapman and Hall. ISBN 402-00341-4/sic/.)

> The author had two purposes in preparing this work: first, as a graduate-level text covering the more common aspects of site investigation procedure and geotechnical design practice, and second as a collection of some 191 design charts and tables used in geotechnical engineering. A background in soil mechanics is assumed. Excellent illustrative matter is provided. Primarily for special libraries in the physical sciences. (RGK)

Encyclopedia of American forest and conservation history. Edited by Richard C. Davis. NY: Macmillan; 1983. 2 volumes, 871p. $150.00. ISBN 0-02-907350-2(set).

Forest history may at first glance appear to be overly specialized for a two-volume encyclopedia. However, Richard C. Davis has done an excellent job in creating one. The forests of North America and the forest products industry have both influenced greatly the development of the present United States, and both are chronicled here in great detail. The encyclopedia consists of approximately 400 articles arranged alphabetically, mostly from 1-3 pages in length, with a detailed subject index in the back. Most of them are illustrated and all but the shortest have bibliographies included. A number of appendices are provided, listing information on National Forests, National Parks, Federal land acquisitions, Federal administration officials, and miscellaneous maps of forest lands. All of the articles seem rather accurate, authoritative, and easy to read. Over 150 contributors worked on this encyclopedia, and it should become the standard reference work on forest history in the United States from Colonial times through 1980. It is highly recommended for all libraries with an interest in forestry or the environment. (DAT)

LIFE SCIENCES

Concise encyclopedia of biochemistry. New York: de Gruyter; 1983. 518p. $29.95. ISBN 3-11-007860-0.

This encyclopedia is basically a translation of the second edition (1981) of the "Brockhaus ABC Biochemie." The translators also updated entries, introduced new material, and added a few references to the literature. Compounds, abbreviations, groups of substances, pathways, processes, and techniques are included; individuals are not. Cross references are numerous, both in the alphabetical sequence and in the text of entries. Most are "see" references: one is directed from "contractile proteins" to "muscle proteins," but in the long article on proteins no "see related" reference could be found to the "muscle proteins" entry. Entries vary in length from one paragraph to several pages, and there are many tables, formulas, and diagrams of biochemical pathways. Some entries give historical background and incomplete references (names and years only) to the primary literature. The preface does not indicate what the editors have attempted to cover or how many entries are provided, but the print is small and the format is two columns to a page, so the impression is given that much information is packed into a small volume. Even with the limitations mentioned and those inherent in compiling an encyclopedia on a field changing as rapidly as biochemistry, this is a worthwhile purchase for most chemistry, biology, and medical libraries. (BW)

A dictionary of epidemiology. Edited by John M. Last. New York: Oxford University Press; 1983. 114p. $18.95. ISBN 0-19-503256-x. (Paperback: $10.95. ISBN 0-19-503257-8 pbk.)

According to the foreword, this is the first extensive compilation of epidemiological terms to be published in the form of a dictionary. It is an attempt to impose some order on the nomenclature of epidemiology, but it is not a guide to usage. Terms and cross-references are arranged alphabetically. Most definitions are brief, and "see also" references direct the reader to related entries. Synonyms, abbreviations and illustrations are included where appropriate, and some references to the primary literature are provided. Individuals important to the development of the field are identified and their contributions briefly described. An editorial team that solicited comments from over 100 colleagues is responsible for the selection of terms and their definitions, and these contributors are listed in the front of the book. A bibliography of sources consulted follows the body of the dictionary. This slim volume will be essential in many health sciences libraries and any library serving public health students or professionals. (BW)

Shepard, Thomas H. *Catalog of teratogenic agents.* 4th ed. Baltimore: Johns Hopkins University Press; 1983. 529p. $35.00. ISBN 0-8018-3027-3.

The new edition of this standard source includes 600 additions, of which 250 are newly listed agents. These agents may be chemicals, drugs, physical factors (such as microwave radiation), and viruses. The compiler has attempted to make this a complete list of all agents that can produce congenital defects and to gather the scattered literature of teratology to link information on experimental teratogenic agents with congenital defects in humans. Some agents are listed that are not known to be teratogenic in recognition of the significance of negative published data.

Entries are arranged alphabetically by the name of the agent. The chemical names used are those in the Merck Index, and there are many cross references from trade names and synonyms. Each entry consists of a short summary of work published, and gives species, dose, age at administration, and type of congenital defects produced. This is followed by a list of citations selected for their currency, originality, or because they are reviews. Quite a few 1982 references are cited. There are separate subject and author indexes, and the endpapers are devoted to a chart of comparative time periods of embryonic and fetal development in humans and experimental animals. (BW)

PHYSICAL SCIENCES

American Association for the Advancement of Science. *1983-84 guide to scientific instruments.* Washington: AAAS; 1983. 225p. $14.00.

A slim but useful tool, this annual guide provides a list of laboratory instruments and equipment to aid in the expansion of instrument usage outside of the field in which the device is currently in use. The directory lists the instruments alphabetically followed by a list of manufacturers. The "category number" is printed to the left of each company name for easy reference to the listing in the next section—the manufacturers directory. Here, manufacturers are listed alphabetically along with their address and phone number. To obtain more detailed information on specific products, "circle numbers" listed on the Reader Service Cards may be used. In addition, the directory contains an advertising index to the main advertising section. (KLB)

Budnitz, Robert J. and others. *Instrumentation for environmental monitoring. Vol. 1: Radiation.* NY: Wiley; 1983. 1130p. $150.00. ISBN 0-471-86880-9 (vol. 1).

Produced by the Lawrence Berkeley Laboratory Environmental Instrumentation Survey, this volume is a treatise on detecting and measuring ionizing radiation. It is divided into twenty chapters arranged in three parts. Part I covers the theoretical background of radiation, its biological effects, and its measurement. Part II details the specific health hazards and measurement techniques used in the nuclear power and uranium mining industries. The third part describes measurement and monitoring procedures for nine commonly used radioactive elements. All of the chapters are state of the art reviews, providing current, authoritative information with extensive bibliographies. Perhaps the most useful section of the book is Appendix A which lists (in nearly 500 pages) currently available equipment for radiation detection and measurement. Any library serving research in environmental or nuclear science will find this volume extremely valuable. (DAT)

Christensen, James J.; Izatt, Reed M. *Handbook of metal ligand heats and related thermodynamic quantities.* 3d ed. New York: Marcel Dekker; 1983. 783p. Price not given. ISBN 0-8247-7030-7.

This compilation was undertaken to aid those working in such fields as chemistry, physics, biology, medicine, and engineering where these data are necessary and useful. The book is a compilation of heats of interaction, ΔH, together with the related thermodynamic quantities log K, ΔS, and ΔCp, where available. The book consists of a Table, in which are summarized the published literature values through 1980 under the headings of the various ligands, and four indexes. This edition contains 1547 separate ligand entries. The criterion for including a metal-ligand pair in the Table was that ΔH values must have been reported in the published literature. Values appearing in theses, technical reports, books, or other nonrefereed sources were not included. In addition to the ΔH, log K, ΔS, and ΔCp values, the following information is included: the appropriate reaction, temperature, method, and conditions of measurement of ΔH; original and additional literature references; and pertinent supplemental information. Empirical Formula, Element, Synonym, and Reference comprise the indexes. The Reference Index includes a year by year alphabetical listing of all references cited in the Table. (CC)

Dictionary of computing. NY: Oxford University Press; 1983. 393p. $29.95. ISBN 0-19-853905-3.

Another entry in the continuing parade of computer dictionaries, but with this one indeed filling a gap in the market. While most of the current dictionaries seem to be aimed at the personal computer/business world, this dictionary is designed for the academic computer scientist. It contains over 3750 entries covering thirteen broad fields from formal languages, grammers and automata to the legal aspects of computing. Coverage is much more extensive for the theoretical and mathematical aspects of computer science than for applications such as office automation or word processing. More than fifty contributors worked on this project from both Great Britain and the United States. The language used in all of the definitions is at a scholarly level and the entries are well cross-indexed. This dictionary is recommended for anyone working on the mathematical and theoretical side of the computer, as well as any libraries supporting such research. (DAT)

Dummer, G. W. A. *Electronic inventions and discoveries.* 3d rev. and expanded ed. NY: Pergamon; 1983. 233p. $40.00. ISBN 0-08-029354-9.

This handy reference tool is basically an updated collection of concise descriptions of some 500 inventions involving electronics, arranged chronologically from 1642 to 1982. (Two non-electronic devices from 1642 and 1672 are included as an essential part of computer history.) Literature sources are carefully cited. Note, however, that invention coverage is only from Europe, the United States, and Japan. Also included as separate chapters are six histories of various aspects of electronics (e.g. radar and television), each including a very clear "geneology" table. There is also an alphabetical list of all the inventors cited, each providing their invention date, and finally a list of 37 publications on inventions and inventors, although some of the older books are out of print. For most academic and larger public libraries. (RGK)

International who's who in energy and nuclear sciences. London: Longman; 1983. 531p. $195.00. ISBN 0-582-90110-3. (Distributed by Gale Research Company, Detroit.)

Part 1 provides professional biographical profiles of over 3800 individuals (alphabetical by surname). Part 2 is a country and topic list of the same people. This work takes a broader and more applied view of energy science than the publication it supersedes, *Who's who in atoms.* For all modern science and technology collections. (RGK)

TECHNOLOGY

Automatic sprinkler systems handbook. Edited by Robert M. Hodnett. Quincy, MA: National Fire Protection Association; 1983. 388p. Price not given. ISBN 0-87765-240-6.

> This handbook is intended to assist in the application of NFPA 13 (1983), *Standard for the installation of sprinkler systems;* NFPA 13A (1981), *Recommended practice for inspection, testing and maintenance of sprinkler systems;* and NFPA 13D (1980), *Standard for the installation of sprinkler systems in one and two-family dwellings and mobile homes.* Contributors to the handbook include members of the Technical Committee who have been responsible for the development of the individual documents. It should be pointed out, however, that the commentary on the text is the opinion of the Editor and Technical Consultants and does not necessarily reflect the official position of the NFPA nor the Committee on Automatic Sprinklers. It is hoped that the handbook will assist fire protection practitioners in obtaining a better understanding, and appreciation for, the requirements contained in NFPA 13, NFPA 13A and NFPA 13D. (CC)

Bostick, Glyn and others. *ASTI: The avoidance/suppression approach to eliminating terrestrial interference at TVRO earth stations.* Syracuse, NY: Microfilco Press; 1983. Mixed pagination. $125.00.

> A loose-leaf format handbook of discussions and data presentations limited to the benefits of TV broadcast and reception which have accrued since satellite technology made the national distribution of live TV more economical and flexible. Heavily illustrated. Subscriptions to quarterly update installments available. For special libraries in the satellite technology industry. (RGK)

Butler, Robert Brown. *Architectural and engineering calculations manual.* NY: McGraw-Hill; 1984. 464p. $19.95. ISBN 0-07-009363-6.

This is a unique pocket-sized collection of mathematical problems that occur during the design of commercial and residential architecture. Design problems include topics such as architectural space, structural members, lighting fixtures, or acoustic assembly. The handy and complete index will quickly refer users to appropriate problems. Best for personal purchase but also valuable in most engineering collections. The author is an architect. (RGK)

Carr, Joseph J. *Linear IC/OP amp handbook.* 2d ed. Blue Ridge Summit, PA: TAB Books; 1983. 356p. $21.95. ISBN 0-8306-0150-3.

This is a reference tool designed primarily for electronic hobbyists by providing detailed information on a variety of operational amplifiers: how they and associated circuits work and how to design such circuits. Good illustrative matter. Best for personal purchase and public libraries. (RGK)

Catalogue of European industrial capabilities in remote sensing. 2d ed. Compiled by Eurospace for the Joint Research Centre of the European Communities. Rotterdam: A. A. Balkema; 1982. 310p. $25.00. ISBN 90-6191-263-6.

This is an updated (but not exhaustive) edition consisting of descriptions of equipment offered by 91 contributing companies from ten European countries, and a summary of activities of each company in the field of remote sensing. The main purpose of this reference compilation is to permit earth observation campaigns to be organized in the short term. For industrial and government libraries which might be so involved. (RGK)

Cushman, Robert F. and others. *The McGraw-Hill construction management form book.* NY: McGraw-Hill; 1983. 407p. $34.95. ISBN 0-07-014995-X.

> Comprehensive in scope and practical in approach, this form handbook presents an analysis of construction management with emphasis on current, prevalent contractual arrangements. It shows how to bring in a building project on time and on budget, and explains what kinds of services should (and should not) be provided for in agreements. Many scores of forms are reproduced covering the vast array of contracts, inventory controls, work orders, and the like. For engineering libraries used by those involved in planning and managing construction projects. (RGK)

Friction, wear, lubrication. Tribology handbook. Vols. 1, 2, 3. Edited by I. V. Krogelsky and V. V. Alisin. Translated by Felix Palkin and Valerin Palkin. Moscow: MIR; 1981. [384p., 280p., 264p.] respectively. $120.00/set. ISBN 0-08-027591-5. (Distributed by Pergamon, New York.)

> A three-volume 1981 translation from the 1978-79 Russian language works which summarizes the results of Soviet research on the friction and wear of machine parts and gives data on lubricants and lub additives for various sliding and rolling contact joints operating under a variety of conditions. Of the 694 literature citations, only 75 were non-Russian and none were later than 1977. For mechanical engineering collections. (RGK)

Graf, Rudolf F. *Electronic databook.* 3d ed. Blue Ridge Summit, PA: TAB Books; 1983. 407p. $24.95. ISBN 0-8306-0138-4.

This is a revised and updated edition (since 1974) on a great variety of information on electronics in the form of well-selected, timely, and practical nomographs, tables, charts, and formuli. Included too is heretofore unpublished material. The data provided are theory-free and for formulae there are no derivations and proofs for the reader to plow through. The tool has been divided into six functional sections: frequency data; communications; passive components and circuits; active components and circuits; mathematical data, formulae, symbols; and physical data. Through this arrangement and the thorough index engineers, technicians, amateurs, and students may locate their needs quickly and easily. For any physical science collection with broad reference needs in electronics. (RGK)

Grimes, Dennis J.; Kelly, Brian W. *Personal computer buyers guide.* Cambridge, MA: Ballinger; 1983. 250p. $16.95. ISBN 0-88410-917-8.

If a "one-stop" guide to the selection and purchase of a personal computer system is needed, this directory is a most worthwhile purchase. Divided into four basic sections, the first fifty pages contains a variety of articles which review the history, hardware, software and several applications of personal computers. The second section discusses the different types of home information services available from three major suppliers—Dow Jones/News Retrieval, Compuserve and The Sources. The next section includes short articles submitted by Apple, Commodore, Radio Shack, MicroPro and Intel describing some of their products. The fourth and largest section provides manufacturers' specifications of software products, peripheral devices and accessories. The "Systems Quick Reference Chart" enables the reader to compare most systems at a glance. In addition, the work contains a detailed explanation of personal computer specifications, a software index arranged by application type, a listing of manufacturers and a glossary. (KLB)

The handbook of antenna design. Vol. 2. Edited by A. W. Ridge and others. London: Peter Peregrinus; 1983. 945p. $121.00. ISBN 0-906048-87-7. (IEE Electromagnetic series vol. 16.)

> This work completes a two-volume set on the principles and applications of antenna design with particular emphasis on developments over the period 1967-1976 (although literature references as recent as 1980 are not uncommon). The first volume (vol. 15 of the series) provides the mathematical background and much data on the design of a variety of antennas, such as the optical and quasi-optical types. In this second volume attention is given antenna arrays, radomes, and antennas in the LF to UHF frequency bands. The indexing is thorough. For most electrical engineering collections. (RGK)

Handbook of electric power calculations. Edited by Arthur H. Seidman and others. NY: McGraw-Hill; 1984. Mixed pagination. $39.50. ISBN 0-07-056061-7.

> This compilation provides detailed step-by-step calculation procedures for nearly 300 problems commonly encountered in the electrical field by engineers and technicians. In twenty sections, the topics covered range from areas such as network analysis, dc and ac machines, transformers, transmission lines, batteries, and even economic methods. Treatment is practical, with little emphasis on theory. Literature references are included with each section. There are no exercises but all the problems provided are solved. For electrical engineering collections but should also be considered for large public libraries. (RGK)

Integrated circuits applications handbook. Edited by Arthur H. Seidman. New York: Wiley; 1983. 637p. $39.95. ISBN 0-471-07765-8.

Because the integrated circuits field consists of many specialties, no single individual can be an expert on all the different types of integrated circuitry. Chapters of this handbook have been written by experts affiliated with such organizations as Motorola, Fairchild, RCA, Signetics, and Texas Instruments. The book features worked-out examples accompanied by step-by-step solution procedures and numerous reference tables. The first section of the handbook deals with digital integrated circuits. Topics covered include transistor logic, integrated injection logic, emitter coupled logic, MOS/CMOS logic families, charge coupled devices, semiconductor and bubble memories, and the microprocessor. The second section of the book is devoted to linear integrated circuits. Topics considered are op amps, active filters, waveform generators, analog-to-digital and digital-to-analog converters, communications integrated circuits, voltage regulators, interfacing circuits, and phase locked loops. The concluding section treats thin film, thick film, and integrated circuit fabrication technologies. (CC)

Japan's electronics almanac, 1983. Tokyo: Dempa; 1983. 305p. $25.00.

Divided into two parts, this work provides comprehensive coverage of the Japanese electronics industry. The first part consists of a series of chapters reviewing industry trends in consumer electronics, electronic parts, computers, peripherals, measuring instruments, semiconductors, ICs, PC boards, materials and displays. In addition, other chapters cover communications, office automation, medical and optoelectronic equipment. Extremely valuable are the detailed statistical tables and graphs depicting various market trends. The second part provides one to four-page summaries of the leading electronics companies. Arranged alphabetically, the outline begins with a brief listing of the company address, phone number, president, date of establishment, amount of capital stock and employees. The main body continues with the history, business philosophy, lines of business, products, future outlook, export trends and overseas investment. Subsidiaries are also listed when available. Essential for keeping up-to-date in a rapidly changing industry. (KLB)

Khashab, A. M. *Heating, ventilating, and air-conditioning systems estimating manual.* 2d ed. NY: McGraw-Hill; 1984. 320p. $37.50. ISBN 0-07-034536-8.

This edition updates (since 1977) considerably the systems data and performance criteria in heating, ventilating, and air-conditioning systems cost estimating. The manual continues to provide a background on the engineering and components of such systems and is replete with charts, graphs, tabulations, and basic illustrations. It is truly a valuable tool for those engaged in preconstruction estimating, bidding, value engineering, or in project cost control. Especially important to appropriate special libraries. (RGK)

Marsh, Paul. *Illustrated dictionary of building.* NY: Longman; 1982. 256p. $33.00. ISBN 0-86095-848-5.

In this work the author has been quite successful in producing a highly practical reference work which is reasonably comprehensive and relevant to what goes on at a building site today. Over 5900 terms (including cross-references) are given but excludes archaic terms and too-highly specialized expressions. Some 800 of the terms include accompanying diagrams. For architects and those interested in the building trades. (RGK)

McGraw-Hill encyclopedia of electronics and computers. Edited by Sybil P. Parker. NY: McGraw-Hill; 1984. 964p. $59.50. ISBN 0-07-045487-6.

This encyclopedia explores the discipline of electronics and the manifold applications of electronic devices, with particular emphasis on computer science and engineering. Coverage is on scientific principles, the science and technology of electronic devices, and their applications. Many of the articles are taken from the *McGraw-Hill encyclopedia of science and technology* (5th ed., 1982)—some updated—and others were written exclusively for this volume. 477 articles (arranged alphabetically) are provided but there is no indication which are the reprints. Excellent illustrative matter supports much of the text. The work is designed as a "first-stop" entry into the world of electronics and should be available in university, business, and public libraries. (RGK)

Riley, Frank J. *Assembly automation: a management handbook.* New York: Industrial Press; 1983. 330p. $39.95. ISBN 0-8311-1153-4.

Automatic assembly as discussed in this reference work is *neither* automation *nor* packaging *nor* mechanism design. It is, however, a systems approach to a reduction in the largest area of direct and indirect manufacturing costs. Too, it is a systematic statement of experiences and observations in the selection, procurement, design, building, and installation of automatic assembly machines made over the past 25 years. Included is an excellent support collection of clear, detailed photographs. For collections stressing production management. (RGK)

Roper, C. A. *The complete book of locks and locksmithing.* 2d ed. Blue Ridge Summit, PA: TAB Books; 1983. 343p. $21.95. ISBN 0-8306-0130-9.

> A very broad-based handbook on locksmithing for the professional as well as the amateur and student of lock technology. The subject is covered from its history through to ultra-high security locks used in military installations. Included is information on various lock mechanisms, locksets, and related tools; data on master-key systems, locks for cars and vending machines, and electrically-operated locks. The considerable illustrative matter is of excellent quality. Best for public libraries and personal purchase. (RGK)

Schwartz, M. M. *Composite materials handbook.* NY: McGraw-Hill; 1984. Mixed pagination. $59.00. ISBN 0-07-055743-8.

> This is a collection of practical information on fibers and metals, their fabrication into a matrix, resin systems, and areas such as composite design criteria, fabrication methodology and related equipment, and quality assurance. A glossary of some 600 items is included. For most engineering and technology libraries. (RGK)

Self, Charles R. *The complete handbook of woodworking tools and hardware.* Blue Ridge Summit, PA: TAB Books; 1983. 392p. $21.95. ISBN 0-8306-0484-7.

> This is not only a handbook but a virtual encyclopedia on what seems to be everything needed for woodworking, from the most basic handtool to stationary power tools, as well as hardware, nails, screws, bolts, hinges, and the like. For example, the index refers to nine different kinds of "saws" and ten references to "bits." The drawings, sketchs, and photographs are excellent and plentiful. Designed for the beginner and intermediate worker, it represents a logical personal purchase and should be in all public libraries. (RGK)

Standard handbook for civil engineers. Edited by Frederick S. Merritt. 3d ed. New York: McGraw-Hill; 1983. Mixed pagination. $79.95. ISBN 0-07-041515-3.

> A considerably expanded edition (since the 2d in 1976) which now also treats new developments regarding environmental control and the use of natural resources, building, and transportation facilities. Emphasis continues to be on fundamental principles and their practical applications. Over one-half of the volume is devoted to specialty fields of engineering, e.g. building, highway, and bridge engineering. Important for all technology and engineering reference collections. (RGK)

Standard handbook of plant engineering. Edited by Robert C. Rosaler. New York: McGraw-Hill; 1983. 1760p. $79.50. ISBN 0-07-052160-3.

> Primarily for plant engineers in a corporate setting who must monitor energy consumption or pollution levels, the handbook is designed to provide data on specific plant equipment along with the planning and construction of plant facilities. Beginning with a glossary and ending with an index, the work is divided into four main sections. Section A reviews methods for site selection and procedures for scheduling, contracting and implementing electric power systems. Heating, ventilating, air conditioning and water cooling systems are also discussed. Section B pertains to the selection and maintenance of plant operation equipment while Section C reviews the tools, processes and materials necessary for operating a maintenance facility. The properties of structural metals and wood are discussed in Section D. In addition, the appendixes include metric conversion tables and a bibliography. A very useful tool. (KLB)

Stein, J. Stewart. *Construction regulations glossary: a reference manual.* NY: Wiley; 1983. 930p. $66.95. ISBN 0-471-89776-0.

A companion to the *Construction glossary,* this volume concentrates on the legal aspects of the construction industry. Definitions are provided for twenty subject categories related to zoning ordinances and building codes. Entries are arranged alphabetically within each category, with an index to all of the categories in the back. All of the definitions have been pulled directly (and apparently unedited) from approximately 500 zoning ordinances, sub-division controls, and building codes. The entries range from short, simple descriptions to complicated legal explanations. Because these definitions have been compiled from so many sources, there are at times many definitions for the same term. For example, under "Lot Line" there are at least 23 different entries, as well as five more under "Lot Lines". This can become somewhat frustrating when looking up a given term, but all of the definitions are ones that are actually in use. Anyone working with the legal aspects of the building and construction industry should find this compilation useful. (DAT)

Telecommunications systems and services directory. Edited by John Schmittroth, Jr. and Martin Connors. Detroit: Gale Research; 1983. 218p. $150.00 for three issue subscription. ISBN 0-8103-1696-X(pt. 1).

This directory permits identification and evaluation of both the traditional telecommunication offerings of established carriers as well as the many new systems and services under development. Coverage includes services such as data communications, satellite services, and voice communications. It is an edition to be issued in three parts for updating purposes. In this first part there are 242 descriptive listings and 224 entries in the glossary (a guide to *general* telecommunication terms and concepts). There are also four indexes: master, function/service, geographic, and personal name. This work is similar to, but does not duplicate, the *Encyclopedia of information systems and services.* For any library—industrial, public, or academic—with even the barest of reference needs in telecommunications. (RGK)

The timetable of technology. Edited by Patrick Harpur. NY: Hearst Books; 1982. 240p. $29.50. ISBN 0-87851-209-8.

More of a coffee table book than a reference book, it provides a comparison of scientific events from 1900 through 1982 and projected into the future. A continuous time line runs through the book, with each year occupying a two-page spread. Six broad topics—Communications and Information, Transport, Warfare and Space Exploration, Energy and Industry, Medicine and Food Production, and Fringe Benefits (Inventions)—are represented on the time chart with important events marked in the appropriate historical location. This provides an easy comparison of events in the history of engineering during this century. There is a subject index in the back to find the year if an event is known. One problem with this book is that it has a very definite British emphasis, and many American readers may be unfamiliar with some of the landmark events represented. Despite this British bias, the "timetable" can be used either as a ready-reference tool or as a book for browsing. It can be useful for a library with an interest in engineering or technology. (DAT)

Todd, Arthur H. J. *Lexicon of terms relating to the assessment and classification of coal resources.* London: Graham and Trotman, Ltd.; 1982. 136p. $55.00. ISBN 0-86010-403-6. (Distributed by Crane, Russak, New York.)

A study of all available conventions and standards generated the terms used in this alphabetically arranged lexicon, translated into English where necessary. However, all foreign language terms are also included as see-references. The original source is indicated in abbreviated form, a full list of such sources being given in an appendix. Most definitions are fairly short, although about 10% are indeed quite lengthy. For libraries in organizations involved in the "supply chain" for coal, particularly in relation to bulk energy supply. (RGK)

Warring, R. H. *Electronic components handbook for circuit designers.* Blue Ridge Summit, PA: TAB Books; 1983. 330p. $21.95. ISBN 0-8306-0493-6.

> This handbook provides the basis for designing a variety of circuits (both standard and integrated) and an understanding of how they work. It is, however, *not* a collection of circuits to build. Included also is coverage of the working principles when using components and how to work out required values. There are a great number of diagrams and the index is most thorough. Best for personal purchase and public libraries. (RGK)

What can be automated? Edited by Bruce W. Arden. Cambridge, MA.: MIT Press; 1983. 934p. $15.00. ISBN 0-262-51026-X(paper).

> This collection of 80 contributions provides an excellent overview of a subject truly suitable for reference collections in electrical engineering and computer science libraries in industrial, university, and larger public libraries. Included in the coverage are statistics, numerical computations, theory of computation, hardware systems, artificial intelligence, programming languages, operating systems, database management systems, software methodology, and applications. This reference tool also defines current research areas and provides projections of possible future developments. Written for the educated layman with some technical background. (RGK)

EXTANT SERIES

Astronomy and astrophysics abstracts. Edited by S. Böhme and others. New York: Springer-Verlag; 1983. 848p. $66.00. ISBN 0-387-12516-7. (Vol. 32. Literature 1982, Part 2.)

This is another volume in a continuing series of semi-annual works started in 1969. It records, summarizes, and indexes astronomical publications (worldwide). Volume 32 contains literature published in 1982 (from over 150 periodical titles) received before February 11, 1983. Some older literature is included. The indexes are indeed comprehensive: 10,360 authors and covers 8826 papers. This tool is quite the ultimate for researchers in astronomy and astrophysics. Well worth the price. (RGK)

Kirk-Othmer encyclopedia of chemical technology. 3d ed. Vol. 23. NY: Wiley; 1983. 979p. $180.00. ISBN 0-471-02076-1.

As a continuation of a vital series, this volume provides coverage for 32 topics ranging from "thyroid and antithyroid preparations" to "vinyl polymers". As usual, the work is heavily referenced and cross-indexed. For all physical science collections in special, university, and public libraries. (RGK)

Sulfur dioxide, chlorine, fluorine, and chlorine oxides. (Solubility data series. Vol. 12.) Edited by Colin L. Young. New York: Pergamon; 1983. 477p. $100.00. ISBN 0-08-026218-X. (For the series: ISSN 0191-5622.)

A compilation of 456 data sheets on solubility of sulfur dioxide, chlorine, fluorine, and the oxides of chlorine in various liquids as given in the primary literature. Excluded are solubilities in molten salts, slags, glasses, metals, alloys, and polymeric material. Literature coverage is to mid-1981. There are two indexes: registry number and author. This volume is one of twelve (with the highest sequence number being eighteen); ten others are in preparation. For virtually every science and technology reference collection in industrial, academic, and large public libraries. (RGK)

SCI-TECH ONLINE

Ellen Nagle, Editor

NATIONAL ONLINE MEETING HELD

The fifth annual National Online Meeting, billed as the world's largest online database conference, was held in New York City April 10-12, 1984. More than 80 papers and talks, approximately 90 product reviews, and over 100 exhibits were featured in the 3-day program. Approximately 3000 persons attended the meetings and exhibits.

End-user systems and use of microcomputers for management of information were major topics at this year's conference. A special exhibit called "Software Village" offered displays of microcomputer software for library and information management applications.

A standing-room only crowd heard industry leaders featured in a panel presentation on "Changing Market Patterns in Online." Martha Williams described highlights of the online database field for 1983. Roger Summit delivered the keynote address at this session, entitled "Online Information Services—A Strategic Perspective." His talk contained a masterful summary of historical milestones in the online field, the current supply and demand of services, and observations about future trends.

Organizers of the conference should be particularly commended for the policy of providing free conference admission to library school students who assist in monitoring conference sessions.

Proceedings of the meeting are available for $50 from Learned Information Inc., 143 Old Marlton Pike, Medford, NJ 08055, Phone: 609-654-6266.

DATABASE NEWS

Access to Major Scientific Databases Altered

BIOSIS is no longer available on the ORBIT system. SDC recently announced the removal of the *BIOSIS* files. Although there are "loyal users" of the files, they were not being used enough to justify maintenance and updating costs, according to SDC. They are however evaluating the feasibility of offering a more streamlined version of the *BIOSIS* files. *BIOSIS* is still available on BRS and DIALOG.

Chemical Abstracts Service (CAS) has refused DIALOG's offer to provide *Chemical Abstracts* abstract text. According to DIALOG, CAS will not be offering the abstract text for license. This significant portion of the *CA* database, will be available only through CAS' own commercial service.

IHS Vendor Information Database Announced

Information Handling Services' *IHS Master Catalog Service* database is now available on BRS. *VEND* as it is called contains full-text information from the catalogs of more than 30,000 vendors of industrial products. Coverage includes architectural engineering, plant engineering, transportation and materials handling, medical equipment and supplies, construction and building products, electrical and electronic engineering, and marine and metric design. Extensive descriptive information on components, equipment, machinery and other industrial engineering products is provided. Each document is vendor specific and contains listings of company names, sales office locations, and available products with brand or trade names. The database may be used in conjunction with the IHS *Military Specifications & Standards* or *Industry & International Standards* databases to find specifications and standards for a given product.

Wiley Catalog Goes Online

The Wiley catalog database, called *Wiley Catalog/Online* is available from DIALOG as File 471. This online version of John Wiley & Sons *General Catalog* contains records for virtually all products published, sold, or distributed by the publisher. It includes books, journals, software, and databases covering a wide range of subjects including business, medicine, computer science, mathematics, architecture, chemistry, engineering, and life sciences.

Records contain full bibliographic citations, descriptions, and tables of contents for the approximately 10,000 items currently in print and available for ordering. In addition, there are approximately 20,000 records describing forthcoming as well as out-of-print Wiley titles. Citations also include basic order information, details on market rights, booktrade discounts and special pricing. All available items can be ordered online through DIALOG's DIALORDER file.

Wiley Catalog/Online will be updated monthly with approximately 200 new records and with updates to the status of existing records. The price for searching is $60 per connect hour and $.20 per full record printed offline.

SEARCH SYSTEM NEWS

SDC Announces Minimum Monthly Charges

SDC Information Services is now assessing a monthly minimum billing charge of $25-$100 depending on the users' service area. These charges apply to all billable services and materials including publications and training. SDC is offering two optional plans for which they will waive the monthly charges.

A Deposit Account Program allows an institution to establish a prepaid SDC account with a minimum $720 prepayment. This may be used over any period of time. If usage (including online connect hour charges, online and offline prints, SDI's stored searches, and telecommunications charges) is under $720 for a 12-month period, there is an additional $60 service charge to carry the account forward.

The $1200 Annual Guarantee Plan may be prepaid in quarterly installments. SDC states that users from the same or different companies may join together under one company account, or join an established consortium account.

SCI-TECH IN REVIEW

Suzanne Fedunok, Editor

SCIENTIFIC PUBLISHING

Urbach, Peter F. The view of a for-profit scientific publisher. *Library Quarterly*. 54(1): 30-35; 1984 January.

In this paper, read at the 42nd (1983) Conference of the Graduate Library School of the University of Chicago on the topic of "Publishers and librarians: a foundation for dialog," the author, who is with Pergamon International Information Corporation, describes how the solutions of librarians and of publishers to the problems caused by increased publishing costs and decreasing library budgets have pitted each against the other.

"Librarians seek to solve their financial problems by resource sharing, networking, photocopying, and more selective acquisitions. Publishers seek to solve their financial problems by price increases and by developing new distribution channels to reach new markets." Mr. Urbach concludes that new technologies such as online systems, document delivery systems and new ways to get access to information will provide solutions to these problems. They will also alter the basic relationships among authors, publishers, librarians, and users.

Pergamon has acquired its own service, InfoLine, in order to serve as a vendor; it wishes to distribute its online products itself. Pergamon participates with an information broker in Berkeley California on the rapid delivery of journal articles. Wiley offers books and journals on-demand through the DialOrder system, and the

ADONIS project is studying the use of optical disk technology to handle single-copy distribution of journal articles. All of these changes with respect to new technologies will have a positive affect on the relationship between publishers and libraries in the future, Mr. Urbach concludes. (1 ref)

Lerner, Rita G. The professional society in a changing world. *Library Quarterly.* 54(1): 36-47; 1984 January.

Rita Lerner, of the American Institute of Physics, presented another paper at the above mentioned conference. In it she explains the difference between how a professional society and a for-profit commercial publishing house regard their "missions." Societies serve their members in many ways apart from the dissemination of information; their publications programs may be not-for-profit in a non-taxed setting. Members are both producers and consumers of the publications of the society.

Much factual information about the AIP is given in the paper; there are tables on the expenses, educational service activities, journal expenses for 1982 (editorial and composition costs accounted for 55% of the total), journal income to the society, and categories of subscribers.

The author discusses recent uses of new technologies at the AIP: composition on ATEX and UNIX systems, recent trials and experiments in document delivery with NASA and with the electronic journal. The ARTEMIS and ADONIS projects are mentioned as of interest to the Institute also. (14 refs)

Petroski, H. A short history of nuclear editing. *Physics Today.* 36(11): 9-10; 1983 November.

In this short article written for the "Guest Comment" column, the author, a director of graduate studies at Duke University in Duram, NC, proposes that following the first self-sustained nuclear chain reaction "the publishing industry quickly discovered the law $E = mc2$, which expressed the observation that a manuscript on atomic energy usually required an amount of editing E equal to the mass m of paper in the manuscript times the author's speed of typing c squared." He gives a brief history of the "Atomic Editing Commission'' (AEC) created in 1946 and of the careers of "nuclear redactors" to the present. (o refs)

Pullinger, D. J. Attitudes to traditional journal procedure. *Electronic Publishing Review.* 3(3): 213-222; 1983 September.

The author, who is with Loughborough University of Technology in England, describes a study he conducted among a group of scientists on their reading and writing habits. The study is part of a continuing effort called the "Blend experiment" to assess the impact of the electronic journal on scientific communication. The same questions on his questionnaire will be asked in four years, after the group has had experience with online electronic communication, and the data will be correlated. (16 refs)

DOCUMENTARY INFORMATION IN INDUSTRY

Vickers, P. H. Common problems of documentary information transfer, storage, and retrieval in industrial organizations. *Journal of Documentation.* 39(4): 217-229; 1983 October.

The author, reporting for the ALSIB Research and Consultancy, describes a project funded by the British Library Research and Development Department to explore common problems in industrial, government, and research organizations both national and international which had come to the Consultancy for help. The author begins with the comment that "it is seldom the shortcomings of the technical information department that loom largest in top management's minds," but his conclusion is that more attention should be given to the efficient operation of the information office in industrial organizations.

A small number of manufacturing firms were studied and a typology of the documents they produced was created (it is shown in a figure in the article), a map of the typical information flows of the firms was drawn, and the author makes comments on the inadequacy of most of the systems studied. The major problems, according to the author, are "corporate memory failure, records management problems, MIS problems, and general management problems." The article concludes with six areas worthy of further study. (13 refs)

Hetherington, J. Computerization of an industrial information department. *ASLIB Proceedings.* 35(9): 358-362; 1983 September.

Mr. Heatherington, of the Howson Algraphy Company in Leeds, England, describes how the STATUS free text information system was used to replace the existing manual system of edge punched cards in his company information office. The transformation amounted to the computerization of the information office itself. The transformation took four years to accomplish, but did not result in any increased staffing or budget overexpenditures. (2 refs)

INFORMATION FOR MANAGEMENT

Ljunberg, S. Intelligence service—a tool for decision-makers. *International Forum for Information and Documentation.* 8(2): 23-126; 1983 April.

The author, who is with the Information and Documentation Center of AB Astra in Sweden, discusses how many innovative and research-oriented industries have made use of the new technologies to develop advanced and effective information systems. At the high levels of decision-making the importance of "paper-borne" information decreases, while the need for intelligence information increases. This problem of how to select and evaluate, and then repackage and interpret "intelligence" reports is key to the success of a documentation center's work. (18 refs)

Green, R. O., Morrison, J. M. and Wantland, R. H. Management Information system for engineering. Oak Ridge Gaseous Diffusion Plant; 30 August 1983. 13 p. DE84001655/CONF-831011131. PCA 02/MF A01.

This technical report discusses the Engineering Management System (EMIS) created to integrate the business management systems of the Union Carbide Corporation Nuclear Division's Engineering division, which is located in three plants Tennessee. The computer-based system keeps track of engineering work load, forecasting, cost, schedule, and selected administrative information. (5 refs)

GATEKEEPER RECONSIDERED

Meyers, L. A., Jr. Information systems in research and development: technological gatekeeper reconsidered. *R & D Management.* 13(4): 199-206; 1983 October.

The authors, who are with the Department of Management Information Science at California State University in Sacramento, California, report on a field study to measure the "selection potential" of an individual as a source of information by his or her colleagues. The study found that there are specialist gatekeepers for each different category of scientific and technological information communicated in the R and D laboratory (project-task information, state-of-the-art information, and research laboratory technique information). This contradicts earlier studies that defined gatekeepers as "global" keepers of all kinds of information. (19 refs)

CYCLE TIMES ON INFORMATION

Kendrick, J. G. Cycle times on information. *Information Society.* 2(2): 97-106; 1983.

This report on the University of Nebraska's AGNET computer system for management information to farmers describes the need felt by farmers to shorten the "cycle times of information," or the time taken for information to radiate from centers of services like banking, legal, and insurance, which require rapid exchange of information out to less populated areas, and then return. The Nebraska computer system is designed to provide this quick information turn-around for the agricultural community. (5 refs)

SCI-TECH COLLECTIONS

Tony Stankus, Editor

It is a pleasure for me to be selected to edit this new section, one which will provide for the publication of descriptions of the key literature on certain sci-tech topics of current interest. It is hoped there will be enough contributions so it will be a regular feature of this journal.

I invite anyone interested in preparing such a paper to contact me so that a quick decision could be made about the publication of a paper on proposed topics. Please address all correspondence as follows: Tony Stankus, College of the Holy Cross, Science Library, Worcester, MA 01610.

A Brief Fermentation Biotechnology Guide to Biochemical Engineering, Industrial Microbiology and Fermentation Literature

Will Jarvis

ABSTRACT. "Biotechnology" usage is examined, and equated with a revised conception of fermentation. Basic, core meaning of biotechnology terminology is considered in relation to such areas as genetic engineering, bioengineering, food-beverage microbiology, biomass conversion and microbiological synthesis. A variety of indexing conventions are compared and a polarity of core *vs* wider applications is posed as a bibliographic consideration. A separate selected bibliography of narrower core treatise and serial titles is presented.

SUBJECT GUIDE

Basic Definitions
and Previous Source Bibliography

This is a subject guide to biotechnology: biochemical engineering, industrial microbiology and fermentation. (These are essentially interchangeable *LCSH* terms.) The scope of this subject guide corresponds basically to *Chemical Abstracts* "Section Heading 16: Fermentation and Bioindustrial Chemistry." Exceptions, corresponding largely to *CA* usage, are noted below. Biotechnology (fermentation) is an ancient technology.[1] The classical definition of fermentation as ". . . the anoerobic metabolism of organic com-

---

Will Jarvis is a science reference librarian at Mart Science and Engineering Library, Lehigh University, Bethlehem, PA 18015, and does online searching and collection development in biotechnology. He holds a BA (philosophy) from Ohio University, an MA (humanities) and an MLS, both from Syracuse University.

pounds by microorganisms or their enzymes to products simpler than the starting material. . ." has been updated to read ". . . any microbial action controlled by man to make useful products."[2] (This Perlman "Fermentation" article is an excellent introduction to today's biotechnology field.) Note that *Chemical Abstracts* 1982 alteration of the old "Fermentation" section heading to now read "Fermentation and Bioindustrial Chemistry" reflects this broadened scope of microbial product research. Biotechnology is a multidisciplinary area with some subject scope pitfalls and terminological confusion. Therefore a rather detailed scope note is in order, including a discussion of selected coverage areas and different definitions of "biotechnology." Collectors unsure of biotechnology's disciplinary scope should examine the prospectus to Verlag Chemie's eight volume *Biotechnology* treatise for a concise outline sketch of the field.

There is only one recent information source title covering fermentation type biotechnology, A. Crafts-Lighty's *Information Sources in Biotechnology,* just published (September 1983) by Nature Press. (This work was not available for review.) H. Rothman's 1981 *Biotechnology: a review and annotated bibliography* has a very sparse bibliography and is quite inadequate for core collection purposes. P. A. Hahn's *Guide to the literature for the industrial microbiologist* was published in 1973, and is becoming quite outdated. The 1963 ACS bibliography *Literature of chemical technology* has a few fermentation and microbiology entries which typify the scope of the older fermentation industry, and is of course very dated.

"BIOENGINEERING" AND "GENETIC ENGINEERING"

"Biotechnology" can also be used as a synonym for biomedical technologies, also known as "biomaterials," "biomechanics," "bionics" or "bioengineering." "Biotechnology" is an *LCSH see* reference to "bioengineering," a term which has a double meaning in *LCSH* parlance. Bioengineering has been used as an *LCSH* subject term for NASA human factors engineering as well as (fermentation) biochemical engineering. The serial *Biotechnology and Bioengineering* for example, is devoted to (fermentation) biochemical engineering and industrial microbiology, not man-machine interactions. A.I.Ch.E. also uses "bioengineering" as a synonym for biochemical engineering. *BIP* (following *LCSH* indexing) uses "bioengineering" in the biomedical-human factors senses of the term, as well as a synonym for microbial production technology research.

"Genetic engineering" is also known as "biotechnology." "Genetic engineering," like "bioengineering" has several different meanings. It is often used to characterize the experimental manipulations of pure molecular genetic research (a.k.a. "biochemical genetics" in *LCSH* and *CA* "Section Heading 3: Biochemical Genetics.") Sometimes the medical "genetic surgery" manipulation of genetic material is termed "genetic engineering" (or "genetic intervention" in *MeSH*.) "Genetic engineering" can also be used more narrowly to mean the applied science of practical, commercially oriented genetic manipulation of microorganisms for chemical engineering production processes. *CA* for example, makes the distinction between ". . . molecular level studies on the structure, expression and regulation of genes, molecular cloning, DNA and RNA mapping. . ." ("Biochemical Genetics") and "Industrial production of a biochemical from cloned genes. . ." "Fermentation and Bioindustrial Chemistry." Since fermentation-bio-technology research literature customarily incorporates specific genetic engineering applications, there is no listing in this core of pure genetic manipulation research, only of specific practical research of microbial production processes. For example, the collected works title *Genetic engineering: principles and methods* is not an industrial applications work, whereas *International symposium on the genetics of industrial microorganisms* 1st-, 1970- is clearly an industrial applications research title.[3] Not all contents are self-evident from titles of course, but the principle is the same.

NARROWER CORE AND WIDER APPLICATIONS POLARITY

Lehigh University's Biotechnology Research Center (and the biotechnology collection of Lehigh's Mart Science and Engineering Library) are typical of generalized biotechnology research operations. (This bibliography began as a collection development study for Mart Library.) Although specific requirements of various biotechnology programs can vary tremendously, most biotechnology collection development programs can utilize the selective bibliography presented below.

It is possible to conceive of wider scope biotechnology bibliographies geared specifically to one or more applications areas; agriculture—forestry, cellulose, food technology, pharmaceuticals, sewage treatment, etc. Obviously, no one such bibliography will completely satisfy a variety of users. Fermentations, unlike chemical processes have ". . . a rather uniform series of techniques. . ."[4] Hence the wide applicability of a smaller core collection. Furthermore, there is the prospect of a broadly construed core collection spilling over into an endless number of product application references, *ie.* steroids or single cell proteins or antibiotics or wood products. Also, since a narrow focus is a solid basis for the addition of special applications references, it is also the best strategy for research centers exploring a multitude of applications (especially since applications possibilities will change over time). Difficulties can also develop in distinguishing (or designating) applications oriented research from basic microbiological or biochemical investigations. For example, enzymes, once known as "ferments," are the "business end" (catalysts) of all microbial production. However, "pure" enzyme research literature, even literature on the immobilizing of enzymes, may not be appropriate for a biotechnologist, when (for example) the uses of previously immobilized enzymes is the researcher's focus.

Biosynthesis, the natural production of chemicals by biological organisms, presents a quandary for the bibliographer of general biotechnology literature. Even "pure" non-economic biosynthesis studies are of a potential interest to biotechnologists. Bibliographers will want to seriously consider *Biosynthesis,* a mostly biannual literature review guide, to keep track of microbiological synthesis literature. Generally speaking, biotechnology is an area requiring very narrower core collections with specific embellishments as *per* local institutional mission requirements.

BIOTECHNOLOGY'S "CLOSE RELATIONS" FOOD AND BEVERAGE MICROBIOLOGY, BIOMASS CONVERSION, AND SEWAGE PROCESSING

A brief parenthetical note is in order regarding several areas related to the core of general biotechnology concerns. The selective bibliography listed in part two below is primarily focused on basic biotechnology, not on these specifics. The field of food and beverage microbiology is closely associated with the development of biotechnology in three ways: not only did fermentation technology have its "cultural" origins (*ie.*, non-scientific) with the fermenting of milk, grains and fruits; today's food and beverage fermentations are still major biotechnology applications.

Furthermore, food and beverage fermentations serve as paradigms for wider biochemical engineering of microbial products, since there is a high degree of uniformity in the various fermentation applications. In fact, *Prescott & Dunn's industrial microbiology,* 4th ed., exclusively utilizes food and beverage microbiological cases precisely in order to provide a definitive treatise of applied microbiological paradigms beyond the food and beverage industries, for general biotechnology applications.[4] In *CA* usage, alcoholic beverage production is covered by the general fermentation section heading, while nonethanolic foods are covered in "Section Heading 17: Food and Feed Chemistry" (*ie.* cheese production).

Biomass conversion (by microbial degradation) of materials such as agricultural wastes, corn, sewage, and wood by-products (esp. cellulose) into fuels, fertilizers and chemical feedstocks has a large and diffuse literature. See for example, the *International Bio-Energy Directory,* or *Energy Research Abstracts* (online as *DOE ENERGY*) or *Bibliography of Agriculture* (online as *AGRICOLA*). Biomass (fuels only, not chemical feedstocks) are covered in *CA* "Section Heading 52: Electrochemical, Radiational and Thermal Energy Technology." Cellulose production is treated under "Section Heading 43: Cellulose, Lignin, Paper, and Other Wood Products."

Fermentation processing of sewage waste is covered in *CA* by "Section Heading 60: Waste Treatment and Disposal." While this microbial processing applications area is not as mainstream as biomass conversion or food and beverage fermentation, it is illustrative of the wide use of biotechnology. The fermentation processing of sewage waste area is also an object lesson in the dispersal of biotechnology applications literature among the various specific applications areas.

FURTHER INDEXING CONSIDERATIONS

Biotechnology titles can hide under a wide variety of subject headings and section headings. *LCSH* and *CA* parlance has been noted above. The very useful review bulletin *New technical books,* by the New York Public Library, requires virtually cover to cover scanning since a wide variety of subject index listings apply there to biotechnology titles. *Ulrich's international periodical directory* and *Irregular serials and annuals: an international directory* also require scanning through general subject headings such as "Biology—Microbiology" and "Engineering—Chemical Engineering" to find specific titles. Online users of *Ulrich's* of course have the advantage of title keyword searching.

BIOSIS PREVIEWS (Biological Abstracts in print) has "Cross Codes" which function like CA Section Headings to provide broad topic classifications, especially useful for online searches. *BIOSIS* Cross Code 39000 is a general "Food and Industrial Microbiology" with more specific Cross Codes such as "39007: Biosynthesis, Bioassay and fermentation" or "39003: Food and Beverage Fermentation."

EIC's *TELEGEN Reporter* utilizes report codes such as: "report Code 02: Industrial Microbiology" for ". . . general discussions and reviews of practical genetic engineering, especially as applied in industry. . . ," "Report Code 08: Chemical Applications" of chemicals that would conventionally be produced by the chemical industry for either general or industrial-speciality purposes. . . ," "Report Code 09: Energy and Mining Applications" which includes biomass conversion, and "Report Code 11: Food Processing and Production Applications." *(TELEGEN* is also available online.)

Microbiology Abstracts: Section A: Industrial and Applied Microbiology, known online (DIALOG) as the *LIFE SCIENCES COLLECTION,* subfile 01, uses a group of section headings including; "Products of microorganisms," "Fermentation and related processes," "microbial degradation," "Food microbiology," "Antibiotics, production and related processes," and "Environmental pollution," (this covers waste disposal as well as related water pollution topics).

CONCLUSION

"Biotechnology," a term with many meanings, is used here to mean the economically oriented research of biochemical engineering and industrial microbiology. Since there are so many microbial applications it is necessary to focus on a narrow core of biotechnology terms and titles. This narrow core concept is extremely useful to the biotechnology bibliographer. Even though no single core can satisfy the diversity of biotechnology needs, such a narrow core can be of use to even the most diverse user populations. Readers are referred to Appendix 1 for a brief chronology of key dates in fermentation biotechnology.

REFERENCES

1. See for example, Høyrup, H.E. Beer. *Encycloedia of chemical technology.* 3:692, 1978 or Hesseltine, C.W. A millennium of fungi, food, and fermentation. *Mycologia.* 62 (2):149-197; 1965 March-April, or the many fermentation references in Tannahill, R. *Food in history.* New York: Stein and Day, 1972. ISBN 0812814371.
2. Perlman, D. Fermentation. *Encyclopedia of chemical technology.* 9:692, 1978.
3. *Genetic Engineering: Principles and Methods.* v.1- , 1979- .New York: Plenum, also International Symposium on Genetics of Industrial Microorganisms. *Genetics of Industrial Microorganisms.* 1st- ,1970- .
4. Perlman, p. 861.
5. Pirt, S.J. Review of *Prescott & Dunn's industrial microbiology.* 4th ed. *Nature.* 299:379; 1982.

SELECTED BIBLIOGRAPHY

The selected bibliography below does not focus on "pure" microbiology, nor on general chemical engineering references. (ISI's *JCR* and OCLC postings of *LCSH* have been consulted to clarify the degree of applications content in particular titles when citations were inadequate or texts unavailable.) The bibliographic entries for applications areas must be strictly limited, since the applications of biotechhnology are now so vast and diverse. The emphasis is on core general biotechnology works, not on diverse applications areas.

TREATISES

The recent proliferation of multivolume to biotechnology treatises has diminished the need to collect biotechnology classics. Only recent, English language treatises are listed.

Atkinson, B. *Biochemical engineering and biotechnology handbook.* New York: Nature Press; 1983. 1119 p. ISBN 0943818028.
Encyclopedia of chemical technology ("Kirk-Othmer"). 3d ed. 1978- . ISBN 0471020753. (Definitive entries include; "Fermentation," "Enzymes, immobilized," "Fuels from biomass," etc.)
Laskin, A.I.; Lechevalier, H.A., eds. *CRC handbook of microbiology.* 2d ed. Vol. V-VI, *Microbial produts.* (In preparation, 1983.) Cleveland, Ohio: CRC Press; 1977- .
Moo-Young, M. et al, eds. *Advances in biotechnology.* New York: Pergamon; 1981. 3v. ISBN 0080253652.
Moo-Young, M. et al, eds. *Comprehensive biotechnology and bioengineering.* New York: Pergamon, 3 v. ISBN 0528680382. (In preparation, 1983.)
Reed, G., ed. *Prescott & Dunn's industrial microbiology.* 4th ed. Westport, Conn.: AVI; 1982. 883 p. ISBN 0870553747.
Rehm, H.J.; Reed, G. *Biotechnology: a comprehensive treatise in 8 volumes.* Weinheim, Germany: Verlag Chemie; 1981- . ISBN 0895730413.

Stewart, G.G. et al, eds. *Current developments in yeast research.* New York: Pergamon; 1981. 682 p. ISBN 0080253822. (Touted as the 4th, companion, volume to *Advances in biotechnology.)*

Vogel, H.C. ed. *Fermentation and biochemical engineering handbook: principles, process design, and equipment.* Park Ridge, NJ: Noyes Publications; 1983. ISBN 0815509502.

Wiseman, A. ed. *Principles of biotechnology.* New York. Distributed by Chapman and Hall; 1983. 217 p. ISBN 0412002612.

SERIALS: ANNUAL AND IRREGULAR

Advances in Applied Microbiology. v.1- , 1959- . ISSN 0065-2164.
Advances in Applied Microbiology. Supplement. no. 1- , 1968- .
Advances in Biochemical Engineering/Biotechnology. v.26- , 1983- . Continues *Advances in Biochemical Engineering.* v.1-25; 1971-1982. ISSN 0055-2210.
Advances in Biotechnological Processes. v.1- , 1983- . ISSN 0736-2293.
Annual Reports on Fermentation Processes. v.1- , 1977- . ISSN 0140-9115.
Applied Biochemistry and Bioengineering. v.1- , 1976- . ISSN 0147-0248.
Biochemnical Engineering Research Reports. v.1- , 1976- . ISSN 0710-0620.
Biosynthesis. v.1- , 1970/71-. ISSN 0301-0708.
Biotechnology Bioengineering Symposium. no. 1- , 1969- . ISSN 0572-6565.
Developments in Industrial Microbiology. v.1- , 1960- . ISSN 0070-4563.
Enzyme Engineering. v.1- , 1972- .ISSN 0094-8500.
Kogyo Gijutsu Biseibutsu Kogyo Gijutsu Kenkyusho Kenkyu Holoku. Report of the Fermentation Institute. v.36- , 1969- . ISSN 0368-5365. Continuation of *Kogyo Gijutsuin Hakko Kenkyusha Kenkyu Hokoku. Report of the Fermentation Research Institute.* v.1-35; 1943-1969. ISSN 0015-0061. Articles in English or Japanese; table of contents also in English.
Progress in Industrial Microbiology. v.1- , 1959- . ISSN 0555-3989.
Reports From the Institute of Applied Microbiology, University of Tokyo, 1961- . ISSN 0082-481X.
Topics in Enzyme and Fermentation Biotechnology. v.1- , 1977- .

SERIALS: PERIODICALS

Applied and Environmental Microbiology. v.31- , 1976- . ISSN 0099-2240. Continues *Applied Microbiology.* v.1-30, 1953-1975. ISSN 0003-6919.
Applied Biochemistry and Biotechnology. v.6- , 1981- . ISSN 0273-2289. Continues *Journal of Solid Phase Biochemistry.* v.1-5, 1976-1980. ISSN 0146-0641.
Applied Biochemistry and Microbiology. v.1- , 1956- . ISSN 0003-6838. Translation of *Prikladnaja Biohimija i Mikrobiologija.* t.1- , 1956- . ISSN 0555-1099.
Bio/Technology. v.1- , 1983- . ISSN 0733-222X.
Biotechnology Advances. v.1- , December 1983- . ISSN 0734-9750.
Biotechnology and Bioengineering. v.4- , 1962- . ISSN 0006-3592. Continues *Journal of Biochemical and Microbiological Technology and Engineering.* v.1-3, 1959-1961.
Biotechnology Letters. v.1- , 1979- . ISSN 0141-5492.
Biotechnology News. v.1- , 1981- . ISSN 0273-3226.
Enzyme and Microbial Technology. v.1- , 1978- . ISSN 0141-0229.
European Journal of Applied Microbiology and Technology. v.5- , 1981- . ISSN 0171-1741. Continues *European Journal of Applied Microbiology.* v.1-4, 1975-1977. ISSN 0340-2118.

Hakkeo to Kogyeo. (Fermentation and Industry.) v.34- ,1976- . ISSN 0386-0701. In Japanese.

Journal of Applied Biochemistry. v.1- , 1979- . ISSN 0161-7354.

Journal of Chemical Technology and Biotechnology. v.29- , 1979- . ISSN 0142-0356. Continues *Journal of Applied Chemistry and Biotechnology.* v.21-28, 1971-1978. ISSN 0375-9210, and *Journal of Applied Chemistry.* v.1-20, 1951-1970. ISSN 0021-8871.

Journal of Fermentation Technology. v.55- , 1977- . ISSN 0385-6380. Contains English language articles, while *Hakkeo Keoguku Kaishi.* v.55- , 1977- contains Japanese language articles. These two journals continue *Hakkeo Keogaku Zasshi.* v.22-54, 1944-1976 and *Jozo Gaku Zasshi.* v.1-22, 1923-1944.

Process Biochemistry. v.1- , 1966- . ISSN 0032-9592.

Trends in Biotechnology. v.1- , 1982- . ISSN 0167-9430.

APPENDIX I

SOME SIGNIFICANT DATES IN FERMENTATION BIOTECHNOLOGY

c. 3000 B.C. Ancient urban civilizations of Egypt and Mesopotamia are brewing beer.

1683 A.D. Leeuwenhoek first describes observations of bacteria.

1856 Pasteur demonstrates that microorganisms produce fermentations and that different organisms produce different fermentation products. (His commercial applications include the "pasteurization" of wine as well as milk.)

1940 Prescott and Dunn's *Industrial Microbiology,* 1st edition is published.

1943 Industrial microbiological production of penicillin begins.

1963 ACS *Literature of Chemical Technology* published. Fermentation industry is still prebiotechnology.

1965 Hesseltine's inaugural address "Millenium of Food, Fermentation, Fungi" published in *Mycologia,* signalling growing influence of industrial microbiology.

1970's Energy crisis promotes microbial biomass conversion, gasohol, etc. Pollution awareness spurs microbial waste processing.

APPENDIX I (continued)

1973	Hahn publishes *Guide to the literature for the Industrial Microbiologist,* a reflection of the field's growth.
1977	Coenzymes, mixed cultures, immobilization are now major enzyme biotechnology topics. *Topics in Enzyme and Fermentation Biotechnology* begins publication.
1978	Perlman's formal redefinition of fermentation as any commercially useful microbial product.
1980	Charkabarty's patent on (a micro) life-form upheld by Supreme Court.
1981	U.S. Congress's Office of Technology Assessment publication *Impacts of Applied Genetics* reports on key issues in genetic engineering and fermentation biotechnology.
1981	Proliferation of Biotechnology Treatises.
1982	*CA* "Fermentations" Section Heading becomes "Fermentation and Bioindustrial Chemistry."
1983	1st volume of new (now multivolume) 9th edition of *Bergey's Manual of Determinative Bacteriology* is published.
1983	*Advances in Biochemical Engineering* changes name to *Advances in Biochemical Engineering/Biotechnology.* Birth of new annual review: *Advances in Biotechnological Processes.*

For Product Safety Concerns and Information please contact our EU representative GPSR@taylorandfrancis.com
Taylor & Francis Verlag GmbH, Kaufingerstraße 24, 80331 München, Germany

www.ingramcontent.com/pod-product-compliance
Lightning Source LLC
Chambersburg PA
CBHW052132300426
44116CB00010B/1865